WRITE. NOW!

A wealth of inspiration and guidance for writers and want-to-be writers

By
Sylvia Dickey Smith

Write. NOW!!
A wealth of inspiration and guidance for writers and want-to-be writers

ISBN: 979–8–9883208–2–1

Cover design by Sooraj Mathew

Edited by Hilary Jastram, www.bookmarkpub.com

GET IN TOUCH

SylviaDSmith.com

syl.dickey@icloud.com

Audible.com

https://www.audible.com/author/Sylvia-
Dickey-Smith/B002ZE9Q8Q

LinkedIn

https://www.linkedin.com/in/sylvia-
dickey-smith-73aa2a8/

Podcast Radio: Writing Strong Women

https://www.blogtalkradio.com/
writingstrongwomen

Other books by Sylvia

https://www.amazon.com/stores/Sylvia-
Dickey-Smith/author/B002ZE9Q8Q

Dance on His Grave

Deadly Sins Deadly Secrets

Dead Wreckoning

Swamp Whisperer

Painted Ladies

Original Cyn

A War Of Her Own

Sacred Lessons From Wilderness Wanderings

Sassy Southern Classy Cajun

In Memory Of...

PHILIP MARTIN, Owner-Publisher of Great Lakes Literary. Much of what I know about writing came from his wisdom, his heart, his love of story.

His words, below, have been taped on my laptop for years.

Make your stories:

Wonderfully Eccentric

Deliciously Detailed

Satisfyingly Surprising

Leave your readers saying:

I'm intrigued

I'm delighted

I'm amazed.

CONTENTS

Preface

Introduction

The Bone Collector

i. Finding Yourself as a Writer

Color 1

You Are Enough 5

How to Write for Yourself. 7

Face The Ghosts 15

Pay Attention 17

What Is This Thing Called Writer's Voice? 19

Find the Heart of Your Writing 29

Exploring Disappointment. 31

Old Dogs, Blue Leopards, & Baubo 33

Writing With Purpose 39

Rules for Writing Fact or Fiction. 43

Writing From the Inside Out 45

Signs You Are Seriously Off-Track. 49

ii. Writing Tactics & Strategies

How Do I Write? 53

What's So Wrong With "to be" Verbs? 71

Don't Play It Safe 75

Three Critical Elements Needed to Write Stories That Rise
      Above the Norm. 77

Spin a Tale, Tell a Story 81

Leave Your Reader Hanging by a Thread 83

iii. Just the Facts

So, What Is This Thing Called "Focus"? 95

How to Create the Flavor of Your <u>Novel</u> 97

What Is Theme Exactly? .101

Plot Is Not 103

Just How Do You Show? .105

How a Sense of Place Influences Your Writing 117

A Cognitive Secret 135

iv. Improving Your Skill

Multi-Dimensional Characters in a
    One-Dimensional World 139

Tips for Applying an Emotional Filter 145

Exploring Your Character's Past 155

A Gift For You

Acknowledgments

About The Author

A NOTE FROM ME TO YOU

I hope you enjoy and find useful this twenty-year collection of presentations written and delivered by me at writers' colleges, conferences, libraries, writers' groups, writers' clubs, workshops, and other opportunities where I was fortunate to discuss my passion for words. I have learned much from so many— writers from all genres, time periods, settings, and workshops. I have made a great effort to share those lessons and resources. From so many, so very much, for which I give thanks.

It is my hope that you might find the key that unlocks your passion for words and the track that shows you how.

PREFACE

Burrowed deep within my psyche, seemingly at the very core of my existence, lives the Story Catcher. I feel I've known her all my life, even before I learned to talk. Perhaps she arrived along with me the day I was born.

I awake most mornings sensing her eagerness, knowing she's worked overtime. I've lived eighty-plus years, and still, it seems she's not yet done with me, not nearly done. So, on I go, following her nudges and her inspiration ... and yes, her nagging does help and inspire.

Her inherent passion for story insists I keep an eye out for just the right word, idea, character, and, yes, perhaps even a bad haircut. I've felt her nudging me in the ribs, whispering in my ear, visiting me in my dreams, and sliding the bedcovers off my legs in the middle of the night as if to make sure I don't miss one of her ideas for a story.

I'm not sure I ever fully embraced the calling to be a writer because I didn't fully understand it. This is a thought that continues to spin in my brain. But today, one month from my eighty-third birthday, she made it clear to me, her voice like a wisp on the wind: "Keep going, Sylvia; you're not done yet."

INTRODUCTION

Our society seems desperate for courageous, dangerous writing ... work that inspires, moves, and resonates. Writing that challenges us to step outside ourselves and move beyond the status quo.

The world doesn't need more safe, tame writing. It needs words that shake the heavens, defy expectations, and offend sensibilities. Isn't that what we long for, anyway?

- To be moved?
- To be forced to grow and change?
- To escape, retreat and find our true selves within the solace of a story?

But someone must go first. Perhaps that someone will be you.

So, what are you waiting for? Let's race! Do what you were made to do. Don't worry about marketing, audiences, or bestseller lists. There's time for that. This just isn't it.

Right now, we need to write.

Rationalizations are good old-fashioned stall tactics. They are fear, speaking loud and clear. Everything will fall into its place. Trust me. Trust yourself. This will work. But only if you brave the heavens. If you write dangerously. Sure, you might disappoint a few people in the process. That's a given.

However, do something you love.

Write for yourself!

Right?

Right, and there is no better place to start than at the feet of the Bone Collector—the mystical crone who weaves stories together from scraps of magic, marrow of story, and the flesh of imagination.

Are you ready to meet her?

Let's go!

THE BONE COLLECTOR

There's an old woman—a wild woman, if you will—who lives in a hidden place that most everyone knows about but few have ever seen. She's hairy and fat and makes more animal sounds than human. She crows and cackles and wails over would-be storytellers, begging them to come to her hiding place and sing along with her, for storytellers are the only company she allows inside.

Folks say she lives in the Texas Hill Country among the limestone slopes of the Llano Uplift. Others believe she's buried near an abandoned well outside Tucson, Arizona. A man said once he'd seen her traveling south in a burnt-out car with the back window shot out. Then a woman said no; she'd seen her standing alongside the highway just outside El Paso, waiting to ride shotgun in the big trucks crossing the desert headed to California. Another woman claimed she'd seen her standing outside her door in the ghetto, taking notes.

She's a wild woman, all right; however, I call her The Singing Bone Collector. Her only work is to wander from here to there, collecting the bones of unfinished or never-told stories, scattered remnants in danger of being lost to the world. She fills her cave with these bones she's collected, bones of delightful yet unidentified characters—both good and bad, of half-done settings, unfinished plots, points of view problems, and a strong sense of place.

She creeps, crawls, and sifts
through dry riverbeds, across
mesas, forests, mountaintops, and
fields of wildflowers, looking for
such bones.

When she has assembled an entire skeleton, put the last bone in place, and the beautiful white creature lays out before her, she sits by the fire and thinks about what song she will sing.

After she decides—after she is sure—she stands over the creature, raises her arms, and sings out loudly. While she sings, the bones begin to come together, the rib and leg bones of the creature begin to flesh out, and fur springs out along its body.

She sings longer, and the creature's tail curls upward, shaggy and strong. The more the Bone Collector sings, the louder the creature breathes. Still, she sings. She sings until the floor of the hill country shakes. And as she sings, the creature opens its eyes, leaps up, and runs down through the canyon. Somewhere, whether by the speed of its running or by splashing its way into the creek or by a ray of sunlight or moonlight hitting it just right, the creature suddenly transforms into a laughing woman who runs free toward the horizon, a published book in her hand.

So, it is said that if you wander the Texas Hill Country near sundown, and you are a little lost and certainly tired, you are lucky, for this wild woman—this Bone Collector may take a liking to you and show you something—something of the soul.

Our stories start with a bundle of bones collected from the

wilds. It is our work to recover the parts. It is a painstaking process best done when the shadows are just right, for it takes much looking.

The Singing Bone Collector shows us what to look for—that indestructible life force—the bones—the foundation of our tales. She promises that our stories will take shape if we sing the songs and call up that life force within us. This singing Bone Collector lives inside the desert of each of us and crisscrosses all nations down through the centuries.

To write the story within us—we must sing over the bones we collect. We must descend into that wild part of ourselves—of great emotion—to capture and create that song. Her whiskers sense the future, and they know the past as well as the present. She has the far-seeing eye of the crone. She simultaneously lives backward and forward in time, correcting for one side by dancing with the other.

This wild woman of Pay It Forward lives within each of us, leaving us the moral obligation—and the delight—to live and write what we perceive or know, or have experienced. To pay it forward, to share what we've learned with others coming along behind. If indeed we have been breathed upon, our stories reflect such.

Whether male or female, young or old, Black or White, I guarantee this old Bone Collector resides deep inside your psyche, patiently awaiting your discovery of the soul bones she holds for you—bones with the potential to be fleshed out, bones to change ourselves and our world. The writer must have the freedom to move, speak, be angry, and create.

Today, that singing wild woman inside of you collects

bones. She is the soul self, the builder of stories. She makes and remakes stories.

Climb up into the cave. Crawl through the doorway or window of your dream. Sift through the sand and see what you find.

Go gather bones.[1]

1. Estés Clarissa Pinkola. *Women Who Run with the Wolves: Myths and Stories of the Wild Woman Archetype.* New York: Ballantine Books, 2003.

i.

FINDING YOURSELF AS A WRITER

COLOR

How It Affects Us & How to Use It in Our Writing

"He tried to imagine the sound of the color red."
~Pete Hamill

Color affects every part of our lives, but so often, we forget there is an amazing world of color surrounding us and, along with colors, a corresponding taste.

Colorology is the science of studying color and the effects color has on us. Colors are, of course, different vibratory frequencies that we perceive as such. Each color/vibratory frequency has its own impact on us, our emotions, thoughts, and moods.[2]

Let's take a look at a few of these characteristics of color, starting with the root chakra, red, and work our way up.

> **RED:** Red raises blood pressure and heart rate, warms, stimulates, expands, activates, gets energy moving, is selfish, depressed, hot-tempered, active, agreeable, extrovert, etc. Taste: pungent (sharp).
>
> **ORANGE:** Orange is optimistic, self-confident, enthusiastic, courageous, self-disciplined, inventive, self-assured, cheerful, good sense of humor, friendly, people-oriented,

---

2. Dennis, Caryl. *Colorology: The Study of the Science of Color.* Clearwater, FL: Rainbows Unlimited, 1995.

suspicious. Taste: astringent.

YELLOW: Stimulating, warming, alkaline, magnetic, stubborn, intellectual, cynical, negative, expanding, good when you need to recall information. Taste: bitter.

GREEN: Green is peaceful, greedy, loving, selfish, responsive, jealous, flexible, stable, secure. Taste: all tastes.

BLUE: Blue is calming, cooking, patient, communicative, restless, creative, depressed. Taste: sweet.

INDIGO: Indigo is intuitive, deceitful, wise, spiritual, forgetful, humanitarian, arrogant, etc. Taste: sour.

VIOLET: Violet is imaginative, intolerant, spiritual, inefficient, sensitive, obsessive, humility. Taste: salt (saline).

WHITE: Purity, angelic, sinless, perfection, void. White smell is manufactured by combining white color and white noise.[3] It is a neutral smell, not pleasant, not unpleasant. Taste: milk.

Colors affect us physically, emotionally, and mentally when they vibrate throughout our entire systems. Scientists have

---

3. "Smelling a White Odor." ScienceDaily. ScienceDaily, November 26, 2012. https://www.sciencedaily.com/releases/2012/11/121126111215.htm.

proven that colors have an effect on our physical bodies. How? By its vibrations entering our bodies—through our eyes, for one.

Without getting too technical or far out, one way energy enters our bodies is through our eyes; it then moves directly to the pineal gland in the middle of our forehead. We've learned that the pineal gland vibrates faster than any other part of our body. This leads to our brain processing information and impressions and creates impressions that influence pictures in our minds.

This is only a sampling of colors, their meaning, and the tastes associated with each. I encourage you to conduct your own research on color, its meanings and impact on mood, and other areas of life. Use color to your advantage. Let it help your readers see and feel the story.

YOU ARE ENOUGH

"The most important day is the day you decide
you're good enough for you. It's the day you set
yourself free."
~Brittany Josephina

As you enter into these next chapters to ingest the insights I share
about writing, remember to bring the influence and aspects of
colors along with you.

You Are Enough

1. You are enough now—not as a perfectible version of you in the future.
2. Everybody always thinks the party is happening somewhere else. Understand that it is happening wherever you are.
3. We have a damaged idea about inspiration—implying something or someone is coming to give us ideas. You generate the ideas.

You Are Enough as a Writer

1. Follow reasonable writing goals; however, good writing is less important than what happened.
2. All writing is autobiographical. That is not the same thing as "Write what you know."

3. What I feel and what I think is true for me in my private heart and is true for everyone else— we are genius.

4. Writing begets writing. Thinking/talking/ reading about writing is not writing.

"To believe that what is true for you in your private heart is true for everyone—that is genius."
~Ralph Waldo Emerson

HOW TO WRITE FOR YOURSELF

"I celebrate myself and sing myself."
~Walt Whitman

The answer to how you find your voice: WRITE FOR YOURSELF.

In my opinion—writing for *yourself* is the only way to begin writing.

You take your audience into account in the editing and tweaking process. You start, though, by writing for yourself.

Sometimes, quite frankly, you just need to write for yourself with no aspirations of publishing anything. This is the best way to build an audience.

I know. The irony is thick.

Writing for yourself allows you to turn off the internal critic and be more sincere in your writing. It unlocks your passion. (This is also attractive to readers.)

Some of my best writing has come from writing for myself. If this idea is foreign to you, here's how I do it:

Examine Yourself

Socrates (and my slight paraphrase) notes that the unexamined life is not worth living (or writing about).

As you sit at your desk, pen in hand or laptop at the ready, ask yourself:

- What upsets you?
- What do you find frustrating?
- What really ticks you off?

Take note of that. Free-write. Spend time exploring the "why" of this.

Type up a few rants. See what it does for your soul. This is merely an exercise to get you started. If it takes you somewhere, let it.

Call Yourself Out

Issue a challenge to *Yours Truly*. In the safety of anonymity, remember that you're writing for yourself here; then, call out some unhealthy or unproductive habit or tendency you have. Don't do it in a self-effacing way. God knows we creatives don't need another self-inflicted browbeating.

Do it in a powerful and motivational way.

This is my favorite way to challenge myself. I try my hardest to be painfully honest about a personal struggle of my own. Some of my most powerful blog articles were written from this place of dissatisfaction with myself.

Solve Your Own Problem

Begin with self-examination. I look at what bugs me—in the world, our culture, and myself—and then realize I probably have the tools to solve that problem. Or at least I know the solution.

Solving problems is, obviously, a lucrative business (look at the self-help section in your local bookstore. If you still have one, that is).

Be careful. Undertake to solve a real problem. Solving your own problem gives you the experience and expertise to help others. You are, essentially, writing your own testimonial. How fun is that?

Okay, now let's get started.

If it's been a while since you've written just for you, or perhaps you've never done this, take some time today, grab a notebook, and start writing.

This is a workout for your creativity. It's not game day; it's practice. You may need to unplug from your blog and other social connections to really make this exercise successful. But it's worth it.

Writing such as this, below, helped me find my voice.

"Who in the world coined the edict in the first place, and why did Steve Harvey or his publisher choose that outdated term for the title of his latest book? I suggest the more appropriate title of Act Like a Woman, Think Like a Man.

"I am weary of staid, boring, limited, constrained, unnatural, inauthentic, affected behavior of acting. What, I ask, is wrong with a woman being a woman?

"Acting connotes phoniness, pretend, trying to be someone we aren't, a role we assume while on a stage. To call someone a lady is editorializing, describing a behavior. Sometimes I act like a lady, but it is not who I am. I am a woman who is not required to always act like a lady. Similarly, a man is a man who is not always required to act like a gentleman.

"I speak from experience, for I pretended to be someone other than myself for way too many years and almost lost the woman behind the mask. Today, I focus on being me.

"I am not opposed to a woman acting like a lady under certain circumstances. Say, when she visits the queen, the quintessential 'lady.' Or when she gets invited to the White House to meet the president and his wife, who, according to her title, must first and foremost 'be a lady.' God, I hope she has time not to be!

"One of my pet peeves is the name

on public bathroom doors that
informs one restroom is for LADIES
and the other for MEN! Why I ask
you, must women act a lady to use
that restroom when men are not
expected to act like a gentleman to
do the same?

"Fair is fair. It should either be
MEN or WOMEN, GENTLEMEN or LADIES."

---

*I firmly believe that writing comes
from the heart and not the head—
or should, anyway. But sometimes,
we lose ourselves in the craft.*

We become obsessed with people's affirmations and what critics think. If you feel more like a wanderer than a leader, it may be time to take a break from the accolades and write just for yourself. You might be surprised at what shows up. Think about the reasons behind your insecurity.

So why *do* you tell yourself or feel like you're not enough?

Quite frankly, you can't help it. In your mind, you see the project in its ideal form. It's what the Greeks referred to as the "essences."

In some ways, you will *never* achieve that level of perfection you see in your mind. It will always seem like something's missing. That's because most art is never finished.

But, when you're beginning as a creative, something else is at play. There's a reason you have that nagging, "never good enough" feeling about your work—because it's *true*.

The problem is this feeling can lead to despair, which can tempt you to quit. And that's the one thing you can*not* do, regardless of how much you think your work sucks.

There is no magic formula for overcoming this feeling of not being good enough. In fact, it's worth *celebrating*. But there *are* a few things you can do to work through this feeling and still get the job done.

When Your Work Doesn't Match Your Expectations

Give yourself grace.
Failure is a gift.
It's your ally.

In this season of life, in which you are less famous than you may be someday, be grateful for the opportunity to fail without millions tuning in. Take advantage of anonymity. Try things you wouldn't dare do if you had a stadium full of fans (and critics). And don't forget to give yourself *lots* of grace.

Forgive yourself when you create something horrendous (because you might). Laugh at yourself. This is all part of the process. It's called "practice" for a reason. See it for what it is and embrace this time of not-good-enough to get better.

Create, anyway.

You're not creative because of the accolades you get. You're creative because you *love* to create. So do what you love, what you were made to do, and try to do it well. Whatever you do, don't wait. Don't hold your work back from the world.

If you keep creating and sharing what you've made, it <u>will</u> get better. I promise.

Be kind to yourself. Stop beating yourself up in front of an audience before you speak. Stop apologizing at the beginning of every blog post.

Your readers didn't pay their money, time, or attention to hear your self-effacing remarks. They aren't causing them to admire you or even pity you. They just make people want to *leave.*

This feeling isn't humility; it's low self-esteem, and it's unattractive. Please *stop* it. This feeling of never feeling good enough is common. I'm not sure that it ever fully goes away. But as a creative, you must learn how to deal with it, or it will destroy you.

At the same time, realize not everyone feels this way. Your feeling of not being satisfied may be a gift if you can see and manage it that way.

Okay.

It's time.

Time for you to write something you're afraid to write. And then *share* it.

Go do what you were made to do.

FACE THE GHOSTS

"Writing is a passion I have never understood,
yet a storyteller is all I have ever wanted to be."
~Ruth Park

Ghosts are fleeting, subtle entities, which makes them more terrifying. We see:

- Sticky haunts – (The leftover material ghosts leave behind after a person has been bombarded with radiation and their organs turn into a liquid called protoplasm.)
- Vague images of disturbing ideas.

When a ghost shows up, we usually run away, click on the TV, and pour another drink while trying to convince ourselves we didn't see it.

Writers can't afford to avoid them. We *choose* to be haunted.

Break into a haunted house. Eyes wide.
Walk through a cemetery late at night.
Call out to spirits and phantoms.
When you discover a specter, don't run. ...
WRITE.
Grab the details ... fast ... knowing how quickly they spook.
Give it life, sinew. Lend it your skin if you must.
Ask its name and wait for it to whisper why it exists.

Write. NOW!

Do not ignore the lessons of the ghosts—for they can help you write with great enrichment.

PAY ATTENTION

Tune Into the World Around You to Become a Better Writer

"Write what should not be forgotten."
-Isabel Allende

An effective writer must pay attention to *everything*. Learn how to tune into life and the world around you—the seen and the unseen. There is so much more to this world and to those who people it than we realize.

Pay attention to the weary-looking clerk checking your groceries. Strike up a conversation by asking how her day has been. If she's tired, ask how many hours she's worked that day. Find something to compliment her on, then notice how her eyes light up, and her back straightens.

Smile and greet a stranger. Strike up a friendly conversation and enjoy their presence.

Pay attention to the trees blowing in the breeze or the layer of frost on the ground. Walk outside at night and look up at the moon.

Notice if someone looks like they need help, then offer it.

Pay attention when that still, small voice inside says, "Slow down, don't drive so fast." Or "let that person in line ahead of you."

Pay attention to your *significant other*. Hear what they say and make sure you understand it correctly. Every day, tell someone you love them.

Pay attention to your own needs and the difference in how you feel when you take proper care of your body.

In other words, wake up to your world. Participate in it. Interact with others. Give of yourself. Care about each other and care about our planet.

WHAT IS THIS THING CALLED WRITER'S VOICE?

How Do I Find Mine?

*"A writer's voice is not character alone. It is not
style alone; it is far more. A writer's voice lines
the stroke of an artist's brush—is the thumbprint
of her whole person: her idea, wit, humor,
passions, rhythms."*
~Patricia Lee Gauch

Finding Your Voice

You may ask: *Do I have a voice?* The answer is yes, of course,
you do.

Every writer has his or her own voice, and every natural
voice has its own way of telling a story.

It is simply the way the writer projects themself artistically.
It's rhythm; it's pace, sense of detail, and anecdote, and if
allowed to improvise—the voice can find the story's content
and form. Natural voice is like a finger pointing at the moon,
but it isn't the moon itself.

It takes time, practice, patience, and work to refine this
voice to tell a story.

But when your natural voice is allowed to lead the way, the
result becomes a story with fire—with spirit.

*We don't find our voice by getting up on a podium, taking a
deep breath, and sounding like a writer.*

We find our voice by being ourselves. By speaking naturally
and then learning ways to sharpen our voice, so it tells a story

that enthralls the reader.

Have you ever said, "I know the story I want to write, but I can't find the voice to write it"?

The natural voice that is yours and yours alone is the best guide to your story's form. Link that with understanding craft, and your voice will lead the way.

Writing is an alchemical process—all one can do is point you in the direction of the cauldrons and let you figure out the way. An alchemical process can be described as a medieval chemical science—a speculative philosophy that aims to achieve the transmutation of base metals into gold or discover a universal cure for a disease. It might also be the means of indefinitely prolonging life or a power or process of transforming something common into something special or uncommon.

Our voice is an ordinary thing. Every writer has one. It is just who you are, projected artistically. It is often linked to our breath, our speaking voice, and the sense of pace you draw on when you are too absorbed in what you are saying to listen to yourself from a distance. It is also linked to your body or dialect.

Voice is how we write when we don't have time or want to take the time to be elegant.

Voice is ...

- The words we choose.
- The pauses in our breath.
- Whether we tell the story quickly, slowly,

gently, or with anger.

When we harness our voice, it can become a powerful tool.

Voice allows us to take readers wherever we want them to go. Even scary places.

It allows us to get our readers to believe anything.

Because it belongs to us, it is often hard to identify.

A search for voice must always involve a willingness to experience what we already know—but in a new light.

Again, pay attention to what is in your everyday life.

You will find an abundance of images and ideas in what you've taken for granted. This receptive approach to the familiar is the beginning of the discovery of voice.

Voice Deals with Sound, Quite Apart from Meaning

- When you write, you subliminally hear the sounds of the words.
- When you speak, you feel the vibrations in your body.

These sounds are connected to a web of meaning, and we can never completely disengage from that web. However, with a bit of practice, we can return to the experience of our voice as an elemental instrument.

In reality, our whole body participates in the creation of voice—and where our voice resides in the body affects the quality of writing. In other words, writing is not just a mental exercise.

A search for voice requires that we involve a willingness to experience what we thought we already knew but in a new light.

Take time to notice:

- Patterns
- Shapes
- Sounds
- Colors
- Objects in your everyday life
- Look at the floor of your closet. (Scary stuff, there, huh?)
- Listen to the words that occur to you just before you go to sleep.
- Notice if a friend or a family member has a fresh haircut/style.
- Notice the plastic bag flapping on the parking meter.

There is much more involved in VOICE.

Still not sure where to start?

No problem. Most of us need help understanding our voice. Go back a few steps and get more comfortable with who you are and what you really want to say before proceeding. Here's a short exercise that might help you.

Find Your Voice:

1. Describe yourself in three adjectives. Example:

snarky, fun, flirty, rude, arrogant, thoughtful.

2. Ask (and answer) the question: "Is this how I talk?"

3. Imagine your ideal reader. Describe him or her in detail. Then, write to him or her—and only to them.

Example: My ideal reader is smart. She has a sense of humor, a short attention span, and is savvy when it comes to technology and pop culture. She's sarcastic and fun but doesn't like to waste time. And she loves pizza.

4. Jot down at least five book titles, articles, or blogs you like to read. Spend time examining them.

- How are they alike?
- How are they different?
- What is it about how they're written that intrigues you?

Often what we admire is what we aspire to be. For example, copy blogger Chris Brogan, Seth Godin, Ernest Hemingway, and C.S. Lewis are admired by many because their writing is intelligent, pithy, and poignant.

5. List your favorite artistic and cultural influences. Are you using these as references

in your writing or avoiding them because you don't think people would understand them? (Don't cut your reader short.)

6. Ask other people: "What's my voice? What do I sound like?" (Make note of the answers you get.)

7. Free-write. Just go nuts. Write in a way that's most comfortable to you, without editing. Then go back and read it, asking yourself: *Do I publish stuff that sounds like this?*

8. Read something you've recently written, and honestly ask yourself: *Is this something I would read?* If not, you must change your voice.

9. Ask yourself: *Do I enjoy what I'm writing as I'm writing it?* (If it feels like work, you may not be writing like yourself.) *Caveat: Not every writer loves the act of writing, but it's at least worth asking.

10. Pay attention to how you're feeling. How do you feel before publishing? Are you:

- Afraid?
- Nervous?
- Worried?

Good. You're on the right track. If you're completely calm, then you probably aren't being vulnerable. Try writing something dangerous, something a little more you. Fear can be good. It motivates you to make your writing matter.

Do you still find yourself asking, *why do I need a writing voice?*

Maybe this will make it clearer ... .

Finding your voice is the key to getting dedicated followers and fans; plus, it's the only sustainable way to write. If you're not you, you'll eventually burn out.

Once you've found your voice, make sure you continue to develop it. It's a discipline that can't be overlooked if you're going to have the impact you desire and one your words deserve.

The bottom line is that there's a lot of noise in the world. If you're going to get heard, you can't just raise your voice.

You've got to set yourself apart, showing you have something special to say and a unique way of saying it.

EXERCISE: Write Something Dangerous

Important: Start writing just for yourself. Not for attention or accolades. *Just to write.*

When we write without concern for popularity or prestige, something strange happens:

More people pay attention.

We experience this when we pursue passion and forsake public approval: Others join us in the journey.

When you do what you love, people will love what you do because we all love the idea of being caught up in an adventure. We love the thrill that danger brings.

This brings us to *you*.

The Risk of Caution

Of course, there's a risk here:

> What if no one cares that you just poured your
> heart into a piece?
> What if people think it's terrible?
> Worse, what if no one pays attention?

What *then?* Well, at least you had fun creating it. And isn't that what we all want more of—work we love, not just tolerate? This is a no-lose scenario.

Often, however, people *won't* ignore you. They won't loathe your writing; they'll *love* it.

Precisely because *you are doing you* when your art comes from someplace deep and true. People will take notice of that sort of thing. So start digging.

Use the below as inspiration.

> *There is a voice inside of you that whispers all day*
> *long:*
> > *I feel that this is right for me.*
> > *I know that this is wrong ...*
> > *No teacher, preacher, parent, friend*
> > *Or wise man can decide*
> > *What's right for you—*
> > *just don't listen.*
> *~Shel Silverstein, "The Voice" Poem, Falling Up*

What Is This Thing Called Writer's Voice?

Writers see the world differently
Every voice we hear, every face we see,
Every hand we touch
Could become story fabric.
~Buffy Andrews, Author

Or, Maybe You Know This One … .
Today you are you
That is truer than true
There is no one alive
That Is Youer Than You
~Dr. Seuss, Happy Birthday to You!

If Those Two Didn't Hit Your Heart, Read This
Finding your voice is
A process
A journey
To the center of you.
~April Erwin

FIND THE HEART OF YOUR WRITING

*"Writing is my shelter. I don't hide behind the
words. I use them to dig inside my heart to find
the truth."*
~Terry McMillan

If we are writing a book, sometimes it takes us a while
to learn what it's *really* about. We think we know—maybe
we think we are writing a book on class distinction or
environmental crimes—but then, in the process, we find, or
sometimes our closest readers reveal to us—that the hot center
is the relationship between two characters.

Once you find the hot heart of your piece—tend it.

How do you tend it?
Feed the fire!
What does that mean?

Bring the details, secrets, characters, and props to
exacerbate the dramatic situation. Sometimes that's the best
way to increase the heat. The fuel you add can be a memory, a
person, or an environmental element. It can be traumatic.

Here are a few examples ...

A drunk sitting at a bar in a drunken stupor, a persistent mosquito buzzing around his head; he's hot and humid.

It might simply be a ringing phone.

Often the heart of your story is hidden under the fire that you keep piling kindling on top of while it smolders.

Writing with purpose and facing the ghosts is not always an easy trail to follow. Take time to circle the cracks within the questions of your work, and delight in the discovery of purpose. Face the ghosts that show up, give them airtime, follow their trail, *find the heart* of your story—and exploit it.

Before you tackle this work, remember the late Kirstie Alley:

> *"It's funny. No matter how hard you try, you can't close your heart forever. And the minute you open it up, you never know what will come in. But when it does, you have to go for it! Because if you don't, there's no point in being here."*

EXPLORING DISAPPOINTMENT

Don't Abandon Your Writing When Things Get Tough!

> *"If there is a secret to writing, I haven't found*
> *it yet. All I know is you need to sit down, clear*
> *your mind, and hang in there."*
> *~Mary McGrory*

Deal With Disappointment

Writing can be a rewarding experience—especially when things go well. But a writer also deals with the ups and downs that come with the tide *and* the title. It's not just about the writing. That can be easy. What isn't always easy is promoting and marketing your work, developing your fan base, and creating public awareness.

When you write, it is like being a parent. Your writing is *your baby*. You protect it and are not always open to criticism from others, right? But even when you want to, you can't abandon it when things get tough.

You have to see it through and keep learning how to make it better. Go at your own pace. Be your own person, and don't let others determine the value of you or your writing. Enjoy your passion. *Keep your spirits high and become the writer you've always wanted to be.*

OLD DOGS, BLUE LEOPARDS, & BAUBO ...

the Stories That Prove You Can Improve as a Writer

*"The most important advice I can offer is
that writing is a craft that you can learn
by practicing. If you keep writing, you will
improve."*
~Lauren Tarshis

Read the following stories and see how you can improve as a writer by examining the themes and asking yourself: *What would I change to make the story mine?*

OLD DOGS AND BLUE LEOPARDS

Not only can old dogs learn new tricks, but leopards can change their spots. You don't believe me? I tell you, it is true. I've *seen* it with my own eyes, for I am that old dog leaping backward over an inflamed barrel. I'm also the blue leopard with big orange polka dots.

In my bio, I describe myself as being born backward—one foot first and left-handed—and seem to have done most things backward ever since. At seventeen and still a

high school junior, I married a
preacher and soon became known
as *the preacher's wife*. Today, it
is difficult to imagine a girl,
barely seventeen, taking on that
responsibility—a kid playing grown-
up. But I sailed along just fine;
any answer I needed to be given by
my husband. He even gave answers to
many questions I never asked.

I started college as a forty-year-
old freshman and gained a degree in
sociology, a master's in educational
psychology, and then a divorce in a
few short years! Five years later, I
got engaged, bought a house, took a
honeymoon in Hawaii, and married in
Las Vegas on the way home.

Are you still with me so far on
this backward thing?

After many years working in the
human services field, I retired
and took on a new career—I wrote
a mystery book that soon turned
into a series of five in the Sidra
Smart Mystery Series, along with
a cookbook to match. Then I wrote

a historical novel set in Texas
during WWII. Soon, I rebranded my
work: WRITING STRONG WOMEN.

That's when my writing began to
take shape. Strong Women had been
my passion for decades before that,
so it all fit perfectly. However,
to remind you not to beat up
on yourself, this took decades
before I publicly claimed that
identity. So, I might write mystery,
historical fiction, or something
else, but whatever I write, it will
feature a strong woman. Of course,
she likely won't start that way, but
by the time I'm through with her, I
guarantee you she will be.

Think that's a reflection of my life?
You bet your patootie it is! I've
learned that it makes no difference
whether you live your life backward
or forward; the important thing
is that you LIVE IT! And never
say never. Never not do something
because you think you're too old,
too dumb, too bright, too whatever.

If you want to do it, go for it.

Write. NOW!

Now, read the following short story to inspire and motivate you to follow your heart, regardless of your age.

BAUBO, THE BELLY GODDESS

A long time ago, before written history, before the patriarchs of the Hebrew people, many civilizations saw God as feminine and revered the sacred act of procreation and sexuality. As a part of this, they made meaning out of their life by honoring and respecting all the different aspects of women. To do this, they created myths and legends that aided them and made sense of who they were, where they came from, what they did, and why.

Baubo, the Belly Goddess, and her stories help us loosen what is too tight, lift the gloom, and bring the body into humor that belongs to the body—not the mind. The body makes us laugh at such things as Mae West's lines. Belly goddess stories cause endocrine and neurological medicine to course through our bodies.

Old Dogs, Blue Leopards, & Baubo ...

Likely you haven't heard about
Baubo before because only one
popular reference to her from
ancient writings has been found.
Her story was likely destroyed over
the course of conquests, but she
has survived as a wild remnant from
post-patriarchal Greek mythology.
Women of my day (the 1940s–1980s)
were taught to be way too serious
and uptight. I lived way too many
years feeling trapped in a world
that said woman caused the man to
commit the first sin.

Now, I say hogwash! Each of us is
responsible for our own sins, or
lack thereof.

Who helped me get there? One cheeky
little goddess named Baubo.

WRITING WITH PURPOSE

"The purpose of writing is to make your mother
and father drop dead with shame."
~JP Donleavy

"Cat: Where are you going?
Alice: Which way should I go?
Cat: That depends on where you are going.
Alice: I don't know.
Cat: Then it doesn't matter which way you go."
~Lewis Carroll, Alice's Adventures in Wonderland

When we write, our purpose is not to get to a specific place in the book. It's to enjoy each step along the way.

Annie Dillard says, "One of the few things I know about writing is this: Spend it all, shoot it all, play it all, right away, every time … give it, give it all, give it now."

Let me make this simpler …

Let's circle the cracks in the questions to get to the core of them.

There are countless ways into our writing. These ways usually involve innumerable questions.

- How do I start?
- Where?
- Who are the characters?
- What shall I name them?
- What's my plot going to be?

These are fantastic questions—because they create cracks. Fabulous cracks—the beauty of our story is often in the cracks created by those questions, not in the questions themselves.

I invite you to circle those cracks made by your questions.

The answers often change, but we keep circling the questions. How do we do that? By writing. By examining the different sides of the questions, the angles, and the cracks.

As Tim O'Brien said, "Fiction's purpose is not to explain the mystery but to expand it."

The Things They Carried

A classic work of American literature that has not stopped changing minds and lives since it burst onto the literary scene, *The Things They Carried* is a groundbreaking meditation on war, memory, imagination, and the redemptive power and purpose of storytelling.

Lots of people write from answers. We've discovered a truth and want to share it. Tolstoy and C.S. Lewis take us by the hand and walk us through a process to learn the truth they learned. That's not bad. Often those are important truths … however … I challenge you—and me—to read and write, not books that lead, but books that don't lead, that allow you to join them on the search, that utter unanswerable questions, which expand the mystery. To lose yourself in books dripping with purpose—and, therefore, power.

Explore authors like Annie Dillard (*Pilgrim at Tinker Creek*, 2013), Elie Wiesel (*Night*, 1955), and Henri Nouwen (*Life of the Beloved*, 1992) to get started.

RULES FOR WRITING FACT OR FICTION

"Learn the rules like a pro so that you can break them like an artist."
~Pablo Picasso

Every writer has his or her own rules for writing. I assume you have heard the secret that—despite what anyone tells you *there really are no rules to writing.*

Well, yes, there are a few basics, like grammar and sentence structure, but even those can and have been broken by many best-selling authors.

The trick is to know the rules, and then, if you break them, do that well enough that it doesn't matter.

That goes for developing character, as well. What I share are my rules of creating and developing character. Others may do it differently and get there by a different path. That does not mean their way is wrong—not if it works.

What I share in this book when I create characters, etc., works for me. Evidently, to a reasonable degree of success because readers talk about how my characters seem like real people, someone they might know and like—or hate—still a compliment!

One of the neatest parts of being a writer is finding your own way to create the very best, most believable characters you can. It is not easy, given that the character does not currently exist.

Yes, they may resemble people you know or be a composite of several, yet much like parents who create a new person, writers create characters that, if done well, live and breathe inside our heads, demanding control over what they say and do.

So, digest the contents of what I offer within these pages—whether you are breathing life into people parading on your pages or presenting an idea backward—and see if they work for you. If not in totality, maybe they will tickle you in parts and pieces. If that happens, then you wasted neither your money nor your time. Above all else, breathe deeply throughout the process. Remember, that is where inspiration resides—within our breath.

WRITING FROM THE INSIDE OUT

*"It ain't whatcha write. It's the way atcha write
it."*

~Jack Kerouac

Conflict, action, resolution, emotion, and showing (versus telling) are the well-known critical elements of writing fiction. Emotion can be the trickiest part of life. It can also be the trickiest part of writing fiction. When a writer does it well, the payoff is a reader identifying with a character or even becoming the character so they can feel what the character feels.

For example, from my historical novel, *A War of Her Own*:

> *"Throughout the day, she struggled with whether to confront Hal. If she did, she'd be forced to do something about it. She knew the tall, red-headed, greener-pastures kind of guy she married would never be content for long, regardless of where he went or who he married. She knew that and married him anyway, and she, a stiff young woman who tied any passion or emotion into the corner of a handkerchief and beat it into submission with a baseball bat."*

Were you able to get inside the character's head and feel what she felt? Did it give you a glimpse of her feelings and insecurities?

Do NOT Forget

1. If the character's emotions are not there, neither is the character.
2. If the character isn't there, the reader isn't there.
3. ... Hint: Neither is the author in a way that satisfies.

Good fiction requires strong emotion, but how does a writer deal with such a tricky element?

A great technique for conjuring such emotion is what author Nancy Holzner calls "writing with an emotional filter." When done correctly, it fully engages the reader inside the character's mind and world.

For example:

Rather than writing neutral descriptions, the author colors the description according to the character's state of mind. This helps to increase identification with the character and brings the reader more fully into what John Gardner calls the "fictional dream."

Emotional filters show how a character feels, thinks, judges, and interprets—instead of telling the reader.

Another example:

Say I look out my window and observe: "Two feet of snow covered the ground." What does that say about my state of mind? *Nothing.*

If I write,

1. "The pine trees bent under a heavy burden of snow."

or,

2. "A pristine white blanket snuggled around the house,"

what happens?

Correct, you get a sense of how I'm feeling as I look out the window, even though *I didn't write a word about feelings.*

That's running the description through an emotional filter.

Our stories have greater impact if we have our character interpret their environment emotionally. Involve the five senses to give your writing sensory texture, then make sure you convey your character's emotional assessment of what she experiences.

The Emotional Filter Is Always Subjective

It presents your focal character's view of your story world, the situation, the other characters, and the conflicts.

When we attach Mr. Character's opinions to his observations and have him make judgments on everyone else's behavior, he not only becomes a stronger character, but our reader will form a stronger emotional bond with him.

Every once in a while, we find ourselves writing a scene through the eyes of our villain or some other unsympathetic character. That's just how it needs to be. He is just like any other character we are molding from clay.

Be sure to make his filter true to him.

Present his warped view in the living color of his hang-ups and destructive agenda. If we do this well, the reader will love reading about him because he will be so compellingly unlikeable. It won't matter that he is the bad guy.

Don't self-edit during the creative process. If we find it difficult to include the subtleties of an emotional filter while writing our first draft, it is best if we write dialogue or action and add opinions and judgments on the second or third time through.

Invest heavily at those places where you have the most control (your own effort and emotion), and reap the benefits when the reader connects emotionally to your characters and loves your story.

SIGNS YOU ARE SERIOUSLY OFF-TRACK

"A writer is someone for whom writing is more
difficult than it is for other people."
~Thomas Munn

If you find yourself struggling with the below, it's time to stop and make a few corrections. Be assured; we have all been there. Don't get hung up on the emotion of how you feel about taking that side road; just find the main drag and get back on it.

- You have no idea who the protagonist is, so you have no way to gauge the relevance or meaning of anything that happens.
- You know who the protagonist is, but she doesn't seem to have a goal, so your readers won't know what the point is or where the story is going.
- You know what the protagonist's goal is but have no clue what inner issues striving for that goal forces him to deal with, so everything feels superficial and dull.
- You know who the protagonist is and what both her goal and issue are, but suddenly she gets what she wants. She might arbitrarily change her mind or get hit by a bus—when this happens, someone else can seem to be the main character.
- You are aware of the protagonist's goal, but

what happens doesn't seem to affect him or if he achieves it.

- The things that happen don't affect the protagonist in a believable way (if at all), so not only does she not seem like a real person, but we have no idea why she does what she does. This makes it impossible to anticipate what she'll do next.

In all of the above instances, the reader will stop reading.

ii.

WRITING TACTICS & STRATEGIES

HOW DO I WRITE?

Any Ol'way I Can

"This is how you do it: You sit down at the keyboard, and you put one word after another until it's done. It's that easy and that hard."
~Neil Gaiman

How do I write?

When people ask me this question, my answer is, "I write any ol' way I can."

Short stories give examples of that. When the mood or circumstances lead, I grab my computer and "tell it like it is," even when the joke's on me. Makes for good practice. Observe how "Any ol' way I can" is manifested in the stories below. I suggest you make notes as you read, then guess how the author borrowed from the "any ol' way I can" approach.

GLASS SLIPPERS & BIG FOOT WOMEN

In a far-off land, east of the sun and west of the moon, a whiney old crone named Drizella sits outside the golden gates of the Queen's Palace, wailing over fate's misfortune. Beautiful in her youth (according to her mother, at least), she'd dreamed of slipping her foot

into the glass slipper, marrying
the prince, and living happily ever
after, raising perfect children
(with a castle full of nannies to
make sure of this), and of course,
wearing the finest of clothes.

But, alas, the slipper had been too
short and her foot too long. Her
one consolation was that neither
had the shoe fit either sister—her
real sister.

The winey crone snivels, wipes her
nose on the sleeve of her ragged
garment, and bemoans the cruelty of
years. Whence came all the wrinkles
and this thin mousy gray hair? Not
to mention her ever-enlarging nose
and ears and the few scraggly hairs
on her chin. Even the "widow-maker"
mistreats her, refusing to return
her tiny waist regardless of how
tight she pulls the laces. Her back
aches. Her sister never calls, and
her sons come around no longer—the
ungrateful lot.

One beautiful sunny day, while amid
her whining, an even older crone

appears with a glow on her face
and a spring in her step—her voice
pleasant, melodic, even. "Why do
you whine, my dear sister? Do you
not know these are the best years
of your life? Too bad you did not
well prepare yourself, else your
step would spring, and your voice
would sing."

"Give me a break," the whiney
old crone exclaims. "What's so
great about getting old, ugly, and
feeble? My back hurts, no one calls
or comes to visit, and should I
venture out, men pass me by as if
unseen." *Whine. Whine. Whine.*

"It is because you spend your
day in front of the mirror that
you whine, my dear. Mirrors only
reflect the outward you, not giving
a chance for inward reflection. You
give insult to the name of crone.
For a true crone does not whine.
Instead, she fills her days with
wisdom learned over the years, with
purpose, humor, courage, compassion
for others, and vitality."

"Vitality?" the whiney crone spat. "I fight to get out of bed every morning. How in the queen's name am I to find vitality?"

"It takes years of work, my dear, and you are way behind. You've wasted your years regretting each one. You fail to feel empathy or compassion or to use your energy and power wisely. As a consequence of such, you have not earned the joy a wise crone discovers with the passing years."

"Okay, smarty pants. You know so much. Tell me what you did that is so different from me. For you, too, longed to wear the glass slipper and failed. You, too, have aged, yet I see young men here at your feet, eager to learn what you know. Why is that—tell me, old crone."

"Dry your eyes, wipe your nose, and lend me your ear."

The whiney crone did just that.

"First off," the beautiful older

crone said, "is to stop that
infernal whining. You must let go
of the idea that if the stupid
glass slipper had fit your big foot,
your life would have been perfect.
The shoe didn't fit your big foot!
Get over it."

"Okay, Ms. Smarty pants, tell me,
how in this world am I supposed to
do that?"

"Stop thinking about what didn't
work. To dwell on anything we have
no power to change is a useless
exercise, and we end up getting
more and more depressed and spend
our days whining about what might
have been.

"The more you whine, the more you
stay stuck in the past—a past you
can't fix. You stay stuck right
there when the prince tries to put
that silly glass shoe on your foot.
That's truly over and done with,
but because you keep whining about
losing out, you're still caught at
that moment in time. Which ends up
helping you find even more to whine

about.

"That was then—this is now. Whining makes you dry up into an old hag. Look in that mirror. Do you see one juicy thing about you?"

The whiney crone looked. She didn't like what she saw. "You mean to tell me these wrinkles might go away if I stop whining?"

"It won't make the wrinkles disappear, but they'll soften. You'll have more energy—a passion for life. Get involved—care about something. Get interested in something—take your mind off yourself and put it on others. Find something funny to laugh about— every day, without fail. If you can't find it, create it—go find a young lover or something." She laughed.

"Yeah, right. Like that's going to happen."

"You never know—but this one thing I can guarantee—it'll put a spring in your step."

"So, that's all I need to do?"

"Goodness no. There's a lot more
to life than that. Grow something.
Crones are good at pruning and
weeding."

"You mean like a garden? I can't do
that, for my back is too stiff, and
my joints ache like a son of a gun.
Every time I kneel, my—"

"There you go, whining again.
Growing something doesn't mean it
has to be planted, my silly sister.
It can be, but other things need
to grow, too. Nurture something—
whether it be a garden or people.
Find something—or someone—
vulnerable—like a lonely child or
a young mother who can learn from
your wisdom. Despite your whining,
you have learned a few things over
the years—which is the wisdom of
the ages—otherwise known as *women's
intuition*. Trust what you know deep
down in your bones. Let that wisdom
bubble to the top. Share it with

those open to receiving it—those
who look for the wisdom of the
ages. Learn to practice patience—
then teach it to the impatient."

"Is that all?" Drizella wondered
how she could remember all these
lessons, let alone do them. "I
should've been taking notes."

The wise, juicy old crone smiled,
for she knew the secret of the HOW.

"By finding your voice, my dear. For
silence equals consent. Crones like
you and me? We speak our minds.
We tell 'em *how the cow ate the
cabbage*—that the emperor is running
around outside nekked. That's how.
Find your voice, use the wisdom of
the ages, grow something, let go of
the past, stop your dang whining,
and laugh—and learn the beauty of
having a big foot."

The End

***

How Do I Write?

ROSIE

(Inspired by *Saturday Evening Post*
cover art. Norman Rockwell
May 29, 1913.)

Rosie pushed her goggles on her
forehead when the supervisor called
her name. She walked forward and
accepted her latest award with
aplomb, pinning it on her chest
alongside the other medals.

Receiving awards for meeting and
exceeding her quota of suitable
tight rivets—in place and ready
to go—were commonplace everyday
occurrences. However, she wore
every award with great pride,
knowing her work performance outdid
any man in the shipyard.

And here folks had said women
couldn't do this type of work that
their place was in the kitchen, the
USO, or wrapping bandages. Well,
she'd shown them all!

She sauntered down the gangplank
amidst catcalls, and "Way to go,

Red!" shouted at her, but she didn't care. She knew they were just jealous of her work performance, which was much better than theirs.

Rosie grabbed her lunch pail, pulled out a ham and cheese sandwich, and climbed atop a thick, wooden post, rivet gun, and all.

Head held high, she looked down her nose at the men below. They could make fun of her all they wanted to, but she wasn't backing down, not for any of them. She'd found her place and was, dang well, staying in it—like it or not.

***

BLUE EGG ON MY FACE

(Sometimes, the joke's on me.)

Early one Fall morning, I hurried out of the shower, threw on my clothes, and rushed to the grocery, not bothering to dry my hair or put on my usual makeup.

How Do I Write?

It's early, I thought; *I won't see anyone I know.*

Not to be outdone, fate caused a chilly wind to blow as I raced through the parking lot. The breeze not only dried my hair but coifed it into that of a wild woman.

Ignoring my usual vanity, I raced through the produce department, grabbing this and that. No sooner had I started than a voice over the PA system requested, "Would the driver of a Blue Honda Fit, with a Purple Heart license plate number *XXXX* please come to Customer Service?"

My car is a blue Honda Fit with a Purple Heart License plate—I was pretty much blamed specifically! *Had someone hit it? What's happened?*

I parked my grocery basket and headed to Customer Service. On the way, I decided there was no reason to go all the way to Customer Service but to go straight to my car. That's where the problem started.

I bustled toward my car, noticing two men standing behind it. I rushed up. "What's the problem?"

"Is this your car?" the first man asked.

"Yes, why? Is there a problem?"

"I don't have a problem, no," he said, "but this guy does." He pointed to the person standing next to him.

"Okay, what is it?"

I looked at my car—and the car in front of it.

The car in front of it? *What about it?*

Lightning flashed.

Although my small car was well within the lines of the parking space, the second man's car, parked in front of mine—faced the same

direction as mine but was nose-
to-nose with a huge pickup truck
parked on the other aisle.

Land-locked.

The lanes were long, and both our
cars fit in the same parking space;
the only thing was, it was evident
he had been there first. In my rush,
I saw what I thought was an empty
parking space, pulled in behind his
vehicle, and hurried inside.

Talk about red-faced.

"I can't believe I did that," I
said, laughing, "but I certainly
can't deny it."

They laughed, too.

"By the way," the second man said,
"how do you like the Fit? I'm
thinking about buying one."

"We love it," I said, explaining
that it was our second one—and how
my grandson walked away with only
scratches from a severe accident in

the first one.

We chatted a little longer, then
I moved my car to another parking
spot—an empty one this time—and
went back into the grocery store.

Meanwhile, he drove out of the lot.

When I got home, I told my husband,
"Somewhere near here, a man is
walking into his house, holding his
belly in laughter, telling his wife,
"You won't believe what this wild-
haired crazy woman did . . . "

On hearing the tale later, a friend
said, "Well, if I'd done something
that stupid, I sure wouldn't tell
anyone."

My response? "Hey, that story is
too funny to keep, even when the
joke is on me."

***

How Do I Write?

THE DAY OF THE IGUANA

A Fairy Tale

Nothing unusual happened today—
unless you count that thing with
the iguana . . .

There I was, sitting on my front
porch with my feet up, minding
my own business, staring out at
a desert full of cacti, creosote
bushes, and tumbleweeds when the
dang iguana wandered up on the
porch. He stood staring up at me,
his long skinny tongue darting back
and forth like he thought I was the
most delicious thing he'd seen all
day.

If you've never seen an iguana
before, those suckers grow big!
Unlike the little pets you see in
stores plopped down in big, plastic
buckets, this guy must've been five
feet long, especially if you count
that yardstick tail he drug up the
steps behind him. I thought I would
mess my britches before I could get
on the other side of the screen

door. But soon as I did, he gives me this pitiful little look that says he's lost his best friend. And I swear a tear ran down his scaly face.

Never one to hurt a guy's feelings, I said to him, "Baby, it wouldn't be so bad if you weren't so god-awful ugly. Look at that skin! You done look like you been out in the sun *way* too long. And those fingernails! Honey, what you need is a manicure."

So up I get to the bathroom, collect my little basket of clippers, emery boards, and cuticle scissors, and march right back out on that porch. Sure enough, he's still there and still looking sad and forlorn. I open my basket and get to work.

I'm here to tell you that iguana spread-eagled on that porch and lay there just as patient as if I was his mama, fixing him a bowl of ramen noodles and tossing in two (not three) ice cubes to cool it off.

How Do I Write?

In no time, I finished my job and
put my things back in my little
basket. I could've sworn the prissy
critter smiled as he turned and
ambled off the porch with the
brightest, prettiest jungle-red
fingernails you done ever seen.

And that was my day—the day of the
iguana.

WHAT'S SO WRONG WITH "TO BE" VERBS?

"Verbs are the most important of all your tools.
Verbs give us the action, and well-chosen verbs
give us the flavor of that action. Although
we can't banish weak verbs entirely, we can
strengthen our sentences tremendously by
watching out for typical be-verb usages and
substituting stronger choices when possible."
~The Writer Mag

To Be Verbs Are:

Am

Is

Are

Was

Were

Be

Being

Been

"To-be" verbs are state-of-being verbs, which means they unduly claim a degree of permanence. For example, "I am hungry." For most Americans, hunger is only a temporary condition.

They claim absolute truth and exclude other views. "Classical music is very sophisticated." Few would agree that all classical compositions are always sophisticated.

These verbs are general and lack specificity.

A mother may tell her child, "Be good at school today," but the more specific, "Don't talk when the teacher talks today" would probably work better.

Talk about vague. For example, "That school is great." You want to clarify the sentence like, "That school has wonderful teachers, terrific students, and supportive parents."

Not surprisingly, "to-be" verbs often confuse the reader about the subject of the sentence. For instance, "It was nice of you to visit." Who or what is the "it?" We have more work to do.

Strategies to Eliminate the" to-be" Verb

- Substitute: Sometimes, a good replacement just pops into your brain. For example, instead of "That cherry pie sure is good," substitute the "to-be" verb "is" with "tastes," as in "That cherry pie sure tastes good."
- Rearrange. Start the sentence differently to see if this helps eliminate a "to-be" verb. For example, instead of "The monster was in the dark tunnel creeping," rearrange to "Down the dark tunnel crept the monster."
- Change another word in the sentence into a verb-For example, instead of "Charles Schulz was the creator of the *Peanuts* cartoon strip," change the common noun "creator" to the verb "created," as in "Charles Schulz created the

Peanuts cartoon strip."

- Combine sentences. Look at the sentences before and after the one with the "to-be" verb. See if one of them can combine with the "to-be" verb sentence, thus eliminating the "to-be" verb. For example, instead of "The child was sad" and "The sensitive young person was feeling that way because of the news story about the death of the homeless man," combine these sentences to read "The news story about the death of the homeless man saddened the sensitive child."

A suggestion to improve your writing in an instant: Go through your manuscript and do a search for each of these *to be* verbs. See how many you can write around. Try to eliminate as many of them as possible. No, you can't delete them all, but set a goal to reduce as many as you can. You will be surprised at how fast your manuscript shapes up!

DON'T PLAY IT SAFE

(It's all about courageous, dangerous writing and letting
your darlings live ... in a sense.)

*"Never take a writer for granted. They are
snipers armed with words. They know how to
aim with sentences, how to fire with paragraphs,
and how to immortalize their kills in verse."*
~Nikita Gill, Writers Are Dangerous People

Don't kill her; chop off her legs

You don't always need to kill *your darling*. Sometimes you just
need to chop off her legs.

I chopped off the legs of mine—and lost 3,000 words of
manuscript. Ahhhhh! Now the plot can move forward.

You know the pain involved if you ever killed or seriously
wounded *your darling*. I still mourn the loss of that beautiful
chapter written from my darling's point of view, knowing all
along it fouled up the plot.

And if you are one of those who refuse to admit you have a
darling, trust me, you do. We all have that character or scene in
our manuscript that, in our humble opinion, is the best writing
on the planet—bar none.

---

*To cut it would cheat the world
of its beauty—never mind that it
contributes nothing to the storyline.*

But our darlings can do more than not add to our story—they can take it away and take over.

I wasn't the only one who fell in love with my darling. Every critique partner who read of the old, countrified woman with this rich, marvelous voice and manner fell in love with her, yet she grew more substantial than my protagonist.

As written, she became story *interruptus*. She enriched the story, yet the early scene from her point of view became another book. So I agonized for days, weeks even—spending hours trying to work around it, knowing I couldn't kill her all along. With advice from a trusted mentor, I finally admitted to myself that I must figuratively *chop off her legs*.

So, instead of killing my darling, I corralled her. I cut the two chapters from her point of view. I revised the manuscript, letting my protagonist carry the plot yet still maintaining *my darling's* personality and manner of speech, allowing her to remain the same strong character we had all fallen in love with.

So, sometimes you must kill your darling; other times, you can chop off her legs and let her live in all her glory.

THREE CRITICAL ELEMENTS NEEDED TO WRITE STORIES THAT RISE ABOVE THE <u>NORM</u>

*"The difference between the almost right word
and the right word is really a large matter. It's
the difference between the lightning bug and the
lightning."*
~Mark Twain

Go ahead and jot down what I am about to tell you. Please refer to it as often as you need.

There are three critical elements needed to write stories that will knock off your readers' socks.

1. THINK *Wonderfully Eccentric*
2. THINK *Deliciously Detailed*
3. THINK *Satisfyingly Surprising*

Let me better illustrate through the power of these examples:

John Hart, *Iron House*, (2011):
Trees thrashed in the storm, their trunks hard and black and rough as stone, their limbs bent beneath the weight of snow. It was dark out, night. Between the trunks, a boy ran and fell and ran again. Snow melted against the heat of his body, soaked his clothing, then froze solid. His world was black and white, except where it was red.
Deborah LeBlanc, *Morbid Curiosity*, (2007):
He had been forced into closets before, but never

by a witch. At least, he thought she was a witch

…

Betty Webb, *Desert Noir*, (2001):

I was admiring the view from my second-story window when the screaming started.

Patricia Cornwell, *Black Notice*, (1999):

My dearest Kay, I am sitting on the porch, staring out at Lake Michigan as a sharp wind reminds me I need to cut my hair. I am remembering when we were here last, both of us abandoning who and what we are for one precious moment in the history of our time. Kay, I need you to listen to me.

Randy Rawls, *Hot Rocks*, (2012):

I had no problem spotting Hector Garcia as he left the office building on University Drive in Coral Springs. Six-two, two-twenty, navy suit with red and white club tie, gray hair in a buzz cut, carrying a tan stressed leather briefcase. Maria Garcia had described her husband right down to his black wingtip shoes. I didn't need the snapshot she provided, but I checked it anyway.

Great classic tales often start with a great hook that is little more than letting us know a tale is beginning.

If you are writing in the mystery genre, you must also keep this in mind.

THINK eccentricity/THINK details/THINK surprise

(The late Philip Martin gives us these words in his book, How to Tell Your Best Story: Advice for Writers on Spinning an

Enchanting Tale.)

> *"Why does your imagination spin to attention when you hear a phrase such as 'Once upon a time'? Although it requires no verbal response, it also signals a beginning, a crossing from our world to an imaginary one, a joining of teller and listener in the wondrous realm of story.*
>
> *"My relatives knew how to spin a droll tale … and taught me that the real pleasure was not in the impeccable logic of it all but in the engagement we all shared in the spinning of the web of words and being caught laughing in the story altogether, and maybe accidentally learning something new ."*

In media res, yes, we start the story in the middle of an action. But notice how it also begins to tell the story. The opening line must be proposed in such a way that, if the teller paused, the listener would say, "Tell me more." The action underway is significant and summed up in a sentence; it calls for the rest of the explanation of what this story is about right up front.

AND this applies no matter what genre you are writing in—even in some cases in non-fiction writing—wherever we can find storytelling.

SPIN A TALE, TELL A STORY

Three Critical Elements That Fuel the Magic of Story

"If history were taught in the form of stories, it
would never be forgotten."
-Rudyard Kipling

I think we all know at some level that good storytelling exists in a world outside of formal structural elements of literature. That it has intangible aspects, like a haunting melody or an enticing fragrance. It exists in imaginary worlds we know well.

We also know that in its simplest form, storytelling involves three things:

- A beginning,
- A middle
- And an end.

Unfortunately, this doesn't always offer us much tangible help. We start. We continue. Then we wrap it up.

But How Can We Do It Better?

By exploring the three key elements that fuel the magic of story, we can sharpen our chops. These elements roughly correspond to each of the three acts in a play—this same beginning, middle, and end. These techniques won't solve all our problems, but if all goes well, they should give us some fairly specific ways to implement and improve our writing.

Do not forget this lesson and apply it to the magic of your mystery work.

LEAVE YOUR READER HANGING BY A THREAD

Tactics for Creating Unstable Situations

"Good horror is built on suspense. Shock has its moments, but it isn't, and should never be, the defining characteristic of the genre."
~Jonathan Maberry

"Put Your Characters in a Risky or Unstable Situation." This expression was used, proverbial, as early as the 1500s, alluding to Damocles, who vexed King Dionysius with constant flattery. The king invited him to a banquet where he found himself seated under a naked sword suspended by a single hair, signaling his insecure position with the court. Pretty unstable!

If You Want to Create an Unstable Situation, Use the Following ...

Setting

Place can play a big role in creating an unstable situation. The overall "mood" of the story can often be built from the setting itself.

In the prologue of *Morbid Curiosity*, Deborah LeBlanc does a beautiful job of creating an unstable situation. She chose her setting—for the prologue, at least—as the house of a woman called Madam Toussant.

Just the name sets, for me, a story that catches my attention. I'm from Cajun country, so anything that rings of such makes me itch to read it!

> *But she gets more specific. We're not just in Madam Toussant's house. We are in her closet. A closet smelling like mildew, dirty underwear, and <u>old blood</u>.*

I don't know about you, but I've never been in a closet that smelled of old blood. Dirty underwear and sweat, sure. Fresh blood? Maybe if someone cut themselves while shaving, but old blood? *No. Never.*

Was I hanging by a thread?
You betcha! I don't even have to know, at this point, what town we're in—that closet caught me.
How about:

- A smoke-filled saloon with a bunch of drunks carrying guns?
- The background murmur of voices and music—in contrast with clipped and suspicious conversations at the poker table.
- The smell of cheap whiskey and perfume.
- A big pile of money or chips at the center of the poker table.
- The shifting glances of the players and the occasional worried or curious looks from bystanders who just know something is about to happen.

At times, place can be used as a ruse, establishing an idyllic setting where the reader expects nothing to happen, and calamity strikes from out of the blue.

We want to use all six senses in creating and describing place.

What does the place look, smell, taste, sound, and feel like? And what does the character's sixth sense—their gut, their intuition, tell them? What is the ideal position to be in? Perhaps you want to expound on the lucky seat at the poker table?

The Players

It is crucial to create strong, believable characters the reader can identify with and care about. Build the suspense greater: "The kid needs to pee, desperately!" The reader must feel they know the protagonist and must identify with him or her on some level for tension to work at its best. We don't know where we are upfront, but we do know it is Cajun/Creole country—and that we have a figurative (maybe literal?) child whose bladder might burst.

We are again in New Orleans—with these elements of story:

- A room full of people, and the writer starting off with a ten-year-old boy named Caster, forced into an utterly dark closet. We know he's not there by choice because of Deborah's verb usage ("forced"). We know this time is different because now, the person outside the closet isn't his stepmother, who often kills chickens for dinner.

- This time, it is a witch killing the chicken.

Okay, I am hooked. For two reasons—one, as I told you, has to do with the setting—what's going on ... That old blood in the closet.

Two, it is critical to create strong, believable characters with which the reader can identify. Once more, the reader must feel they know the protagonist and must identify with him or her on some level for tension to work at its best. It's the difference between driving by a horrible car accident where you don't know anyone involved and driving by one where you recognize one of the cars as belonging to your loved one.

The protagonist should be both unique and universal. Unique in that she is different enough from the reader that she becomes a "real" person, an individual. Universal in that she must experience the same emotions, the same thoughts, and the same basic goals and needs of the reader so that the reader can relate to what she is experiencing.

Protagonists should also possess the necessary traits and/ or talents to emerge triumphant in the end, but these must be carefully built and established early on in the overall story.

The Deal

In poker, the deal that essentially sets the scene creates the situation that must be (excuse the pun) dealt with and lays the groundwork for tension. Let's apply this to our burgeoning story.

- What cards will you deal to your protagonist?
- What cards will you deal to your antagonist?
- How quickly will the entire hand be revealed?
- Will the reader know what cards are held in each hand? (Address the point of view and keep it consistent.)
- Can the hand be improved upon?
- If so, what decisions and/or actions must be taken to make the hand better?

The Stakes

What is "at stake" in your story? What is the conflict? Everyone wants to win, but only one person (or side) can. The question then becomes:

- How much is each character willing to "bet" or risk to be assured they will win?
- What is the protagonist's ultimate goal?
- What about the antagonist's?
- What steps must the protagonist and antagonist take to reach those goals?
- What obstacles or threats must the protagonist and the antagonist beat to achieve those goals?
- What does each risk in the process?
- When do you up the stakes?
- Are the stakes global in nature or individual to these characters?

The Play

First, you must establish the rules of the game.

- Cheating is allowed, but do too much of it, and the reader will catch you, and you're out of the game.
- Fate or luck can play a small role, but play should be more about finessing the game or gaining the psychological edge.
- The pace of the game is also important. You want to move from tension to high tension quickly, then sustain the high tension as long as you can.
- If too much time occurs between the two, the reader forgets what created the tension in the first place.
- If too little time occurs between the two, tension never has a chance to build.
- Use the structure of your writing to build tension.
- Shorter, more hard-hitting sentences, strong, active verbs, and fast-paced action all contribute to the reader's sense that something big is about to happen.
- Bluffing is an option, of course, but use it sparingly, or the reader will catch on.
- Bluffing can take the form of red herrings or the use of the "sigh, then die" technique where the protagonist anticipates a threat, the tension builds to its maximum, then nothing happens.

- As soon as the protagonist (and the reader) are breathing a sigh of relief, thinking the threat of danger has passed, that's when the danger hits. Careful and sparing use of this technique will keep your readers on their toes and wary—which keeps them turning the pages.

Win or Lose

- Conflict leading to confrontation is the basic skeleton of suspense.
- Use strong, active verbs.
- Contrary to the saying, winning or losing does matter just as much, if not more, than how you play the game.
- If your protagonist doesn't emerge triumphant in the end, the reader will generally feel cheated. But that doesn't mean the protagonist can, or should, win every hand. People love to root for the underdog. The art is in what victories you choose to give her and if they are plausible.
- The protagonist needs to reach an "all is lost" moment when things seem too far gone to ever turn around. But if the protagonist has learned from his losses, studied his opponent, and adapted to the situation, he will find a way to win in the end. It may mean the ultimate gamble—winner takes all.

Write. NOW!

To Create a Plot That Leaves Your Readers Hanging By Thread
Answer the following questions to keep your readers engaged, gasping, and guessing at what's coming.

- Who is involved?
- What is at risk?
- Where is it taking place?
- When will it occur?
- Why is it happening?
- How will it be resolved?

Letting the reader try to figure out any one of these elements can create suspense. Trying to guess *how* it's going to be done can be just as much fun as trying to guess whodunnit.

A Few General Rules

- Show, don't tell—use dialogue and action to convey the story.
- Don't insult the reader with quick, unrealistic, or contrived solutions.
- Know your facts and do your research.
- The reader must care about whomever and whatever is at stake.
- Threats can be physical, emotional, or psychological.
- The antagonist should be fascinating, riveting, fun-to-watch (Think Hannibal Lechter in *Silence of the Lambs.* We were all hanging on

at this villain.)

- The pace of suspense is like a roller coaster ride—first the build-up, then the exciting plunge, then another build-up ...

iii.

JUST THE FACTS

SO, WHAT IS THIS THING CALLED "FOCUS"?

"I generally concentrate on work for three or four hours every morning. I sit at my desk and focus totally on what I'm writing. I don't see anything else. I don't think about anything else."
~Haruki Murakami

FOCUS is the synthesis of three elements that work in unison to create a story:

- *The protagonist's issue:* It isn't so much about whether the protagonist achieves her goal or not; it's about what she must do to attempt to overcome it.
- *Theme:* What does your story say about human nature? The theme needs to be reflected in how your characters treat each other. It defines what is possible and what isn't as the story unfolds. It is what determines whether the protagonist's efforts will succeed or fail, regardless of how heroic she is.
- *The plot:* The events unfold so we can anticipate where the story is heading. This is crucial because "minds exist to predict what will happen next." We love to figure out, and we don't like being confused. It keeps us on the planet longer.

Focus is of utmost importance. The protagonist's issue and

the theme are the lenses through which we determine what the events (plot) will be.

It will chronicle by setting the parameters and zeroing in on the particular aspect of the protagonist's life. (You can cherry pick here.)

HOW TO CREATE THE FLAVOR OF YOUR <u>NOVEL</u>

(Hint: It's more than setting, writing, sensory experiences, etc.)

"All you have to do is write one true sentence.
Write the truest sentence that you know."
-Ernest Hemingway

Some of what we talked about earlier are present here, as I have learned through this wacky and wonderful world of writing that these elements have many different applications. Setting affects character, of course. But setting must also come into play actively. I explain more below.

Writing Senses

When writing the five senses—not yours but those of your characters—they must always be present tense.

You can't STOP your story through every changing backdrop and location to describe a person, place, or thing. No, you must tell on the run. Focus on your character ON THE MOVE.

You must talk about the gunmetal gray skies of Chicago, sure, but do so at the moment your character notices it as he or she is in action.

The Setting Is a Spicy Ingredient

The setting is not just important to a novel. It is the *backbone* of the work. It encapsulates both character *and* plot. Unless an author captures the flavor of the setting, the work becomes bland, a watered-down version—an imitation of story.

- A setting done well puts the reader into the time and place of the story as nothing else can.
- It makes the difference between telling a story or taking your reader on an exciting journey.
- Some (probably most!) writers start with a plot or characters in mind, then decide on the setting.
- As an alternative, try picking out your setting first and then develop your characters and plot within that setting.

If this isn't resonating with you, take heart, as there is no one right way to begin.

Develop your story in a way that works for you. The key ingredient is that you are in love with your setting, whether it is a real place, one you create in your mind, or a mixture of both. If you can't fall in love (or hate) with your chosen location and period, don't cheat your reader by settling. Go back to the drawing board.

How To Create The Flavor Of Your Novel

The Flavor of a Setting

So ... How *do* we capture the flavor of a setting and weave those flavors into the story?

We capture the flavor of a setting by tapping into the senses and then some!

- But remember, less is more.
- These snippets must be interwoven judiciously throughout the story so that the reader isn't even aware that is what you have done.
- Too much too quickly, and you create an "info" dump that ends up boring the reader, and they skip over it. Keep it brief and well thought out.
- If possible, go to the town and dig around. Do what your protagonist does, *within reason,* of course.
- Taste what they taste, hear what they hear, touch what they touch.
- Become a sponge. Soak in as much of the setting as possible until you become the setting and the characters. Fictitious locations can be pretty effective, but they are a little more challenging because you must start from scratch and create rather than simply describe them. The good news is we can do this by tossing elements of several different settings in a big pot, flipping that switch, and watching a new world evolve!

Remember, taste, touch, smell, hear, see—and don't forget the magic of color.

While showing can be difficult, you need to learn how to do it because readers love it! It puts them smack in the middle of the action and lights up their senses!

Before you jump into your story with both feet, take a minute, tromp around in some puddles, and write an example of the show compared to tell. Doing this will put you into good and nimble practice—priceless!

Telling is one of the most challenging habits to eradicate from your style. I still struggle with it. You might be surprised to learn that even some of your most favorite beloved authors do.

Do remember: Writing that shows is so much more interesting than writing that tells. It's worth doing the work.

WHAT IS THEME EXACTLY?

"They say great themes make great novels, but what these young writers don't understand is that there is no greater theme than men and women."
~John O'Hara

Theme boils down to two incredibly simple tenets:

- What does the story tell us about what it means to be human?
- What does it say about how humans react to circumstances beyond their control?

The theme often reveals your take on how an element of human nature—loyalty, suspicion, grit, and love—defines human behavior.

The real secret to theme is that it's not general; it wouldn't be "love" per se—rather, it would be a very specific point you're making about love. (That it's cynical, lyrical, quirky, manipulative.)

When you know the theme of your work in advance, it helps—because it gives you a gauge by which to measure your character's responses to situations.

Theme reveals the POINT your story is making—and all stories make a point, usually beginning on the first page, but not always.

More importantly, what is it I want my reader to walk away thinking about? What point does my story make? How do I want to change the way my reader sees the world?

PLOT IS NOT

What It Is and What It Isn't

"I always begin with a source of inspiration that comes from nature. The story comes from my research, volunteering, and meeting the people involved in that story world. I am an intuitive writer, and an image, sound, experience can all inspire a scene or a plot twist."
~Mary Alice Monroe

Don't bury your story in an empty plot.

PLOT IS NOT: WHAT THE STORY IS ABOUT!!!

PLOT IS: A STORY ABOUT HOW THE PLOT AFFECTS THE PROTAGONIST.

- Plot facilitates story by forcing the protagonist to confront and deal with the issue that keeps them from achieving her/his goal.
- The way the world treats your protagonist and how he reacts, *that* reveals the THEME.

What the protagonist is forced to learn as he navigates the plot—*that* is what the story is about.

PLOT IS: Cause and effect. Stimulus and response.

PLOT IS: The structure of events within a story and the casual relationship between them. There is NO PLOT

CASUALTY!

"Captain Kirk piloted his spacecraft to the stars and back" is an event with no plot. "Captain Kirk piloted his spacecraft to the stars to escape a collapsing world on Earth," etches out the beginning of a plot. To develop it, the author must complicate, complicate, complicate.

JUST HOW DO YOU SHOW?

"Don't tell me the moon is shining; show me the
glint of light on broken glass."
~Anton Chekhov

Welcome to the deeper dive into the age-old (and for a good reason) rule" "Show. Don't tell."

As much as we writers hear this phrase, we seldom receive a good example of how to do that. I did provide peeks into these in another chapter, but I want to really paint a picture for you here.

Common Questions Around Showing

- Is there only one way to "show" a scene?
- Is there a "best" way?
- Is there a secret to doing this well?

To answer these questions, let's turn to film techniques. Cinema embodies the ultimate in showing instead of telling. Even in scenes where a character talks about what is happening, whether the character is on screen or in a voiceover (when you just hear someone talking but don't see them), you still see an event unfolding on the screen before you.

In a novel, if the author interrupts the present action to explain something (narrative or exposition [describe]), the reader stops "seeing" what's going on.

Today, film editors cut, splice, and create scenes out of

numerous segments from different camera angles. Pay attention the next time you watch an action movie. See if you can count all the individual cuts and camera shots that have been pieced together in a segment. Sometimes there are dozens—forcing your eye to shift from close-up to zoom, to panning the action, to an inserted detail, and the list goes on.

If we approach our scenes in a similar fashion, we will produce powerful, riveting backdrops the reader can't take their eyes off.

These scenes don't have to be high-action. Any scene benefits from this technique.

Many novel scenes feel like the camera is stuck in one spot watching what is happening, and that can make a scene flat and boring.

Imagine two people talking while they sit and drink tea, with the camera only showing their faces. Snoozefest.

But you don't just want to "move your camera around" randomly; this is where the secret comes in. You have to know how to hide the rabbit in your hat before you can present your trick to the audience.

Now, pay attention because I am about to reveal all.

Just How Do You Show?

The Secret to "Show. Don't Tell"[4]

- First, remember: Every scene needs to have a point, or it shouldn't be in your novel.
- Second: Every scene needs a *high moment* where that point is made.

We remember great scenes because they contain a great moment. Often that moment is not something huge and explosive. On the contrary—the best moments are the subtle ones in which the character learns or realizes something that may appear small to the outside world but is giant in scope to them.

Once you determine the "moment" in your story, think about the best way to show it.

If you are revealing something small—like a word, an expression, reaction, or a physical detail, you'll want to have your "camera" up close.

If it's a big explosion in a city center, you'll want to use a long shot to see the impact on a huge scale. Once you envision that moment and how you mean to show it, you can work backward to build up to it and give it the greatest punch.

Watch how movie directors tell a story on the big screen using camera shots.

---

4. @KMWeiland, K.M. Weiland. "Structuring Your Story's Scenes, Pt. 5: Options for Scene Disasters." Helping Writers Become Authors, December 20, 2022. https://www.helpingwritersbecomeauthors.com/2013/01/structuring-your-storys-scenes-pt-5.html.

Pay attention to the key moments in each scene and notice how the filmmakers "show" instead of "tell."

If you study great scenes in movies, you can discover ways to fashion great scenes in your novels. Don't be surprised when readers keep saying to you, "Wow, I could really picture your novel as a movie." That is a compliment.

A Challenge

"Show, Don't Tell" Without the Sense of Sight.

When done well, even when an author doesn't describe any physical attributes to you, I bet their words will conjure up a picture in your mind anyway.

When you picture how a scene might play out in this way, your other senses come alive—no matter what you are thinking about. Maybe your sense of smell shifts into overdrive when you imagine losing your sight.

You might transport yourself back to your musty old student room where you burnt incense day and night, or maybe you're imagining a cozy old coffee shop filled with the warming scent of hot drinks.

Notice we haven't used our sense of sight yet. We can probably agree that "sight" is the most used sense in writing. It is the most obvious, anyway.

Writing without sight means exposing the reader to a scene via their emotions and sensory organs. It's transporting them to a specific moment and dropping them right into the middle of it. It's creating a three-dimensional setting rather than giving a rundown of what's visible in the immediate surroundings.

We know that writing is simply a cluster of words on a page.

Just How Do You Show?

Writing doesn't have a deep, aesthetic quality like a painting, so, as writers, we must engage the reader's senses and encourage them to paint a picture in their mind.

When writing, you want the reader to envision an entire scene coming to life simply through your words.

But we don't want them just to imagine it—oh, no—we want them to *feel* like they're actually there in the midst of the action.

Well, our memories are tapped into our senses, and a trigger of these senses floods whole scenarios back into our minds.

Think about it this way: How many times have you not been able to describe how a place made you feel, but you can vividly remember the smell and the sounds? How many times has a fleeting smell jogged your memory, but you can't quite put your finger on where the memory took place?

It's the same with writing.

The reader can connect their memories of smells, sounds, tastes, and touch to situations you've written about, bringing them closer to the story (ergo, putting them in the middle of the action) and making it more meaningful to them.

And that's the ultimate aim of writing, isn't it? To make people feel something.

Now close your eyes for a moment.

Do you notice that your other senses become more attuned? This is replicated in writing that doesn't offer any physical descriptions. The reader's secondary senses become stronger, which allows them to fill in the gaps.

How to Successfully Pull Off Not Using Sight

Write. NOW!

Consider these two paragraphs:

```
The blue sky hung overhead, light
and airy and as fresh as the white
canopies that shaded the grills.
Long, flat fish lay limply across the
bars, turning from a shiny silver
to a charred brown in no time
at all. Underfoot, the concrete
walkway glared with the brightness
of the midday sun, just a few
steps from the white sand that
disappeared out into the blue sea.
```

And now this one:

```
The warmth of the midday sun hung
close, making clothes sticky and
foreheads sweat. Nearby, the gentle
lapping of the waves mingled with
the chirrup of birds flying overhead
and distant chatter. Someone
laughed loudly, cutlery clattered,
and the buttery smell of grilled
fish whirled upwards on the light
breeze.
```

What are you thinking of after that?

The first paragraph paints a fairly comprehensive picture of scene, but it feels two-dimensional, don't you think? The second paragraph encourages the reader to fill in the gaps. What kind of setting do they picture with the sound of waves, birds, and the smell of grilled fish?

It's easy to see how you can use all the senses but sight when you put two paragraphs describing the same scene together like this.

Remember:

- Put yourself in the scene. What can you hear? What can you smell? Relay that information.
- Get tactile. Touch objects you're trying to describe (if you can, get your hands on them) for first-hand knowledge.
- For every scene, try and drop in a descriptor for each sense.

Here's another example where I describe an object of interest.

```
The box was small and brown.
On top, there was a rectangular
white label filled with thick black
writing that had smudged at the
edges. Each side was framed with
sloppily applied gray parcel tape.
```

And:

```
The box had smooth surfaces
interrupted with the bubbly bump
```

```
of parcel tape. It was heavy to
hold and smelt like musty old
photographs and faraway lands.
When it moved, there was a soft
tap, tap, tap, and a low scratching
sound like claws on carpet.
```

Which description is more intriguing?

It's not difficult to use all the senses when writing, but sometimes we forget and find ourselves hung up on the way things look—which is very normal for all of us! Writing without sight is a skill worth practicing that will enable you to bring worlds to life and place your reader where they're supposed to be—right in the center of the action.

A good piece of writing transports the reader, and to do that, you need to engage all the senses—not just sight.

How about you?

Which senses are your favorite to write?

Sensory Exploration

In all cases, a reader should have a full sensory experience. Read this excerpt taken from *Daughter of the Howling Moon* (2015) by Ruth Weeks.

> *"Benjamin tried to pull me up from the deep hole. Every day he'd show me another small wonder of his house. Water with only a turn of a round knob. Light with a flick of a switch. Coffee from a pot plugged into the wall. Oh, and best of all,*

*an inside bathroom with a washtub and a special
contraption that rained buckets of hot water down
my neck and back. Soap that didn't strip the hide
plumb off you. Flowery smelling stuff to wash my
hair with."*

With this paragraph in mind, jot down a few answers
alongside the questions below (or write down your thoughts on
a sheet of paper).

1. What do you see?
2. What do you hear?
3. What do you smell?
4. What do you feel?
5. Where are you?
6. What do you taste?
7. What does this one paragraph tell us about the
   point of view character
8. Does this give a full sensory experience?
9. Is anything missing? If so, what?

Our characters must, let me repeat, *MUST* experience the
world they live in, just as we do, with their senses.

Let's say you write a book set in the 18th century, and
your character stands in the kitchen. She should smell and
feel that food in her hands as she feels and smells the heat of
the kitchen. When a writer describes the same scene, he or she
should stimulate the readers' senses with relevant words that
cause senses to peak. How does a writer indicate to the reader
that the kitchen is hot without saying "the kitchen is hot'?

How about…

- Stifling heat caused by an old wood-burning stove.
- Crackling embers of the open fire …
- The smell of her sweat.
- Her dirty, damp hair dangling over the bread dough as she kneads it with rough hands and dirty, chipped fingernails.
- The smell of three-day-old garbage in the wooden barrel near the door.
- The big, dented, un-scrubbed pots and an old cracked wooden ladle.
- The bright morning light that streams through the broken shuttered window.

"Okay," you say, "the sensory detail above is all about setting, not character. I bought this book to learn about character. How do I flesh out my character within that setting?"

We're getting to that!

Another Example of Sensory Exploration:

In the book, *The New Ones of Atlantis* (2006) by Judy Prudhomme, her character, Lord Priest, says, "One must look in order to see."

Lord Beast says about his father:

"Father's Seer Gift is not something he can simply turn off and on. However, he has told me that he

has to look in order to See. That means he must have the intent of Seeing before he can know and See what others cannot."

Maybe you noticed, but before we can talk about our characters seeing, we must experience that in their setting for ourselves.

Deepen Your Character's Perception of Their Surroundings—An Exercise

Take a character in one of your books, works in progress, or one you dream of writing someday, and walk yourself through these steps:

- See them in your mind.
- Feel them.
- Where are they?
- What does your character see? Describe everything about their environment.
- Describe his or her feelings about what or who she/he sees.
- What colors are there?
- Is it cold or warm?
- What do they smell?
- Is the smell pleasant or unusual?
- Does the smell remind them of anything?
- Is anyone else there? If so, describe them as completely as you can.

Now, quickly, before they leave, does this character remind you of anyone you know in your present life? If so, make a note of it here or on a sheet of paper.

When I ask if there are any smells you recognize, you might find that you cannot answer without actually using your own sense of smell—or the memory of such. Slowly and with patience, ask your character to use all their sense, one by one. Help them. Once again:

- What do you see?
- What do you feel?
- What do you hear?
- What do you taste?
- What do you smell?
- What emotion can you sense?

HOW A SENSE OF PLACE INFLUENCES YOUR WRITING

"You Could Make This Place Beautiful"
~A memoir by Maggie Smith

Not Only Setting but Sense of Place Influences Our Writing

The Sidra Smart mystery series is set in Orange, a small Southeast Texas town said to carry its own gravity. You either get out early, or you don't get out at all.

I got out early—shortly after high school—and that was many years ago.

When I started writing the first draft of *Dance on His Grave* (number one in the series), my husband was adamant: "Do not set the book in Orange, Texas."

You see, he isn't from Orange. Isn't even Texan. His hometown is in South Florida. Add to that, he traveled the world during his thirty years in the Army, so Orange holds no magic for him—gravity, either. He jokes he would only move there when he lost the will to live. He further jokes that everyone who lives in Orange and can read—all ten of them—has copies of my books.

However, when my muse stomped her foot and refused to work with me if I didn't follow her lead, I learned really quickly to do what she says.

I set my books in Orange and never regretted that decision.

In case you are not familiar with that part of the world, traveling east on Interstate 10, Orange is the last get-off before crossing into Louisiana.

Mystical swamps, bayous, and the Sabine and Neches Rivers meander through a part of the state that sleeps under the threat of hurricanes. Where mosquitoes seem as big as dragonflies. Where crawfish boils, and Cajun music entices and entertains.

Setting is not just important to my writing. It is the backbone of the work. It encapsulates both my characters and my plot. When I fail to capture the flavor of that setting, my writing seems bland, watered down—an imitation of story.

My goal is to capture a sense of place and weave it into the setting by tapping into the senses. I judiciously lace snippets throughout the story in such a manner that the reader isn't even aware that is what I have done. As I stated earlier: Too much too quickly, and I create an info dump that ends up boring the reader—the last thing I want to do.

The setting is important, but equally so is a sense of place. It sets the stage. It confines the characters. It forces interaction.

If you struggle with how-to, try having your character reflect on their surroundings. This can fire up the character's passions and fuel their actions. The story and the theme grow deeper and richer. And as always, practice, practice, practice.

Using Place to Show or Develop Character

In Willa Cather's 1913 novel *O Pioneers!*, the story is set in the town of Hanover and out on the surrounding Nebraska prairie.

How A Sense Of Place Influences Your Writing

The main character, Alexandra Bergson, is a tall, strong young woman of twenty at the novel's start. She lives on a prairie farm with her immigrant parents and three younger brothers. All changes when her father falls ill and, dying, entrusts the farm to Alexandra.

Here, at the end of the book's third chapter, is a quiet pause as Alexandra sits on the back stoop and looks out at her land. It sketches in a few details of the prairie setting, but note how Alexandra sees it through her own special eyes, giving us a glimpse into her strong personality, full of intention.

> *"That evening, after she had washed the supper dishes, Alexandra sat down on the kitchen doorstep while her mother was mixing the bread. It was a still, deep-breathing summer night, full of the smell of the hay fields. Sounds of laughter and splashing came up from the pasture, and when the moon rose rapidly above the bare rim of the prairie, the pond glittered like polished metal, and she could see the flash of white bodies as the boys ran about the edge, or jumped into the water. Alexandra watched the shimmering pool dreamily, but eventually, her eyes went back to the sorghum patch south of the barn, where she was planning to make her new pig corral."*

This kind of information about a character in other stories might be revealed through a conversation with a best friend. Here, the land is Alexandra's friend, indeed, her love. We discover her character by seeing how she pauses to relax and reflect on the beautiful, ever-changing, and ever-challenging landscape.

Use Place to Anticipate Mood

Well-placed, evocative description of place is a simple way to foreshadow what is to come. This stems from the reader's awareness that the author is selecting details carefully, so a textured description of place is suggestive of what lies ahead.

Throughout the novel *Watership Down* (1972), author Richard Adams often uses descriptions of place, seen from the point of view of his protagonists (rabbits), to begin chapters. Each passage sets a mood: concern, hope, change. It is generally little more than a faint background cue, like soft music in a film. But the rabbits are sensitive to their environment, so we become ultra-sensitive too.

> *"It was early morning, and the rabbits were beginning to silflay [to graze], coming up into clear gray silence. The air was still chilly. There was a good deal of dew and no wind. Five or six wild duck[s] flew overhead in a swiftly moving V, intent on some far-off destination. The sound made by their wings came down distinctly, diminishing as they went away southward. The silence returned. With the melting of the last of the twilight, there grew a kind of expectancy and tension as though it were thawing snow about to slide from a sloping roof. Then the whole down and all below it, earth and air, gave way to the*

sunrise. As a bull, with a slight but irresistible movement, tosses its head from the grasp of a man who is leaning over the stall and idly holding its horn, so the sun entered the world in smooth, gigantic power."

Something the writer is suggesting is about to happen.

Use Place as a Setting for Action

Almost any description of action, whether a barroom brawl or a drive across town, requires a keen sense of place. If the setting is complex, whether a small town or even a house more than a few rooms, many writers find it helpful to create a map, to understand the spatial geography of the characters' movements.

All action scenes ask the reader to visualize what is happening so that we can imagine the hero swinging from the chandelier, then crashing against the small table in the dark corner of the bar.

But beware not to get bogged down with too much detail. Especially in action scenes, the details of place need to be crisp and appropriate to the pace of the scene.

We note this done well in *Across the Nightingale Floor* (2002) by Lian Hearn.

"The dark bulk of the castle loomed in front of

us. The cloud cover was so low that I could barely make out the highest towers. Between us and the fortification wall lay first the river, then the moat … We slipped one by one into the river and swam beneath the surface to the far bank. I could hear the first patrol in the gardens beyond the moat. We lay in the reeds until it had passed, then ran over the narrow strip of marshland and swam in the same way across the moat.

"The first fortification wall rose straight from the moat. At the top was a small, tiled wall that ran all the way round the garden … Kenji dropped onto the ground to watch for patrols while Yuki and I crept along the tiled roof to the southeast corner …"

"I knelt and looked upwards. Above me was the row of windows of the corridor at the back of the residence. They were all closed and barred, save one …"

There are, of course, some places that characters are afraid of, as found in any horror or gothic novel. In other cases, the characters are deeply in love with the place they call home.

Again, from *O, Pioneers!*:

"Alexandra drew her shawl closer about her and stood leaning against the frame of the mill, looking at the stars which glittered so keenly through the frosty autumn air. She always loved to watch them, to think of their vastness and distance, and

of their ordered march. It fortified her to reflect upon the great operations of nature, and when she thought of the law that lay behind them, she felt a sense of personal security. That night she had a new consciousness of the country, felt almost a new relation to it. (...) She had never known before how much the country meant to her. The chirping of the insects down in the long grass had been like the sweetest music. She had felt as if her heart were hiding down there, somewhere, with the quail and the plover and all the little wild things that crooned or buzzed in the sun. Under the long shaggy ridges, she felt the future stirring."

Alexandra has fallen in love with the Nebraska prairie. As she does, so do we.

Help Your Character Develop a Relationship With Place

If your setting is to have a "sense of place," the characters in your work should feel it first and foremost and deeply.

Is Scarlett O'Hara simply the owner of Tara, or is she in a more complex relationship with her home?

For her, place is far more than just a physical space to be inhabited. It is something that she interacts with on a deep emotional level. As one of the great writers of place today, Barry Lopez, winner of the National Book Award, wrote: "Many of us, I think, long to become the companion of a place, not its owner."

Allow the Place to Come to Life

With a great character, his or her role might grow beyond mere description or involvement in plot. At some point, such a character might begin to speak on his or her own behalf, affecting the course of the story in unexpected ways. In short, a great character becomes alive.

Likewise, the place in your work can come alive to achieve what might be called "there-ness." There-ness is the sense of awe, impact, and respect that we (and the characters in the novels) have for the prairie in *O, Pioneers!* or *Cannery Row*—Steinbeck's novel, or for the great north in Jack London's tales or the barn in *Charlotte's Web*.

How does a writer create there-ness? In the same way you allow a character to come alive: listening carefully to what the place really is, at its core, beyond the superficial stereotypes. Although a great place is not a person, it can come to life if you allow it to.

Mostly, this happens as an act of listening and caring. You can achieve it if you spend time with the place in your story and permit it to have its own voice instead of just being a stage to step upon.

As Marjorie Kinnan Rawlings wrote in *Cross Creek* (1952) about a country road:

> *"Folk call the road lonely, because there is not human traffic and human stirring. Because I have walked it so many times and seen such a tumult of life there, it seems to me one of the most populous highways of my acquaintance. I have walked it in ecstasy, and in joy it is beloved. Every pine tree,*

every gall berry bush, every passion vine, every joree rustling in the underbrush, is vibrant.

"I have walked it in trouble, and the wind in the trees beside me is easing. I have walked it in despair, and the red of the sunset is my own blood dissolving into the night's darkness. For all such things were on Earth before us, and will survive after us, and it is given to us to join ourselves with them and to be comforted."

In the words of another writer, Paul Gruchow, writing of the Boundary Waters canoe country in northern Minnesota, describes the difference between scenery and place:

"Scenery is something you have merely looked at; place is something you have experienced. (...) This voyage into place ultimately leads toward memory, the great leavening agent of our lives."

To be a better writer, look for ways to develop a sense of place. Think of how to make the place someplace that a reader would want to visit and linger in, to enjoy being a companion for a while, of that special place that anchors your story. A great sense of place can set your story apart. It will offer new kinds of insights into the characters. It can test them, support them, change them. It is, as Paul Gruchow said, the great leavening agent—that will make your stories rise above the rest.

Write. NOW!

Create a Sense of Place

> *"Every story would be another story, and unrecognized ... if it took up its characters and plot and happened somewhere else."*
> *-Eudora Welty*

What do great stories do?
They take you to another place.

Place is where everything happens. But it is not just a platform for stage action. Place influences stories far more than many realize.

Think of great novels you know and love. For instance, consider the role of Hogwarts in the *Harry Potter* series. From the beginning, Hogwarts plays a tremendous role in the story. It is the place where magic is learned and friendships formed. More than that, Hogwarts stands for what must be saved; it represents the ideals of those who practice magic for the good. With its strange denizens and ever-changing hall, the school of wizardry is a powerful thread linking the multi-book series, as each installment follows Harry and friends through another year. If Hogwarts were not so unique, the *Harry Potter* series, despite its endearing characters and complex plot, would be more commonplace.

Place also plays a key role in nonfiction. Consider how place (the "where" of a story) helps shape the elements of who, what, and even why. Good journalists know that painting an evocative picture of a story's setting always draws readers into a scene and creates an aura of authenticity.

In short, stories that lack a "sense of place" seldom advance from the depths of the slush pile. In contrast, stories with a strong sense of place do.

Let's look at steps to build a stronger sense of place in your stories.

When describing a key place for the first time, choose a point of view.

First, you must choose whether you will present the place from an insider or outsider point of view. Is this a place your main character knows well, or is it newly encountered?

Charlotte's Web (1952) is a wonderful story, delivered in E.B. White's beautiful prose. In it, most conversations between Wilbur the pig and Charlotte the spider take place in a barn. This place is first introduced with the following lyrical passage, written from the point of view of someone who knows the barn very well.

> *"The barn was very large. It was very old. It smelled of hay and it smelled of manure. It smelled of the perspiration of tired horses and the wonderful-sweet breath of patient cows. It often had a sort of peaceful smell—as though nothing bad could happen ever again in the world. It smelled of grain and of harness dressing and of axle grease and of rubber boots and of new rope. And whenever the cat was given a fish-head to eat, the barn would smell of fish. But mostly it*

smelled of hay, for there was always hay in the great loft up overhead. And there was always hay being pitched down to the cows and the horses and the sheep.

"The barn was pleasantly warm in winter when the animals spent most of their time indoors, and it was pleasantly cool in summer when the big doors stood wide open to the breeze. The barn had stalls on the main floor for the work horses, tie-ups on the main floor for the cows, a sheepfold down below for the sheep, a pigpen down below for Wilbur, and it was full of all sorts of things that you find in barns: ladders, grindstones, pitchforks, monkey wrenches, scythes, lawn mowers, snow shovels, ax handles, milk pails, water buckets, empty grain sacks, and rusty rat traps. It was the kind of barn that swallows like to build their nests in. It was the kind of barn that children like to play in. And the whole thing was owned by Fern's uncle, Mr. Homer L. Zuckerman."

E.B. White starts with short sentences and builds slowly, introducing the sense of tired, sweet patience. We encounter diverse scents and learn who shares the space (cat, cows, horses, sheep). But there is almost no visual description until the second paragraph when the big doors are thrown open. Then we see details: the organization of the stalls, the clutter of objects. Finally, it is summed up as a warm and enjoyable place for animals and children alike.

Imagine, on the other hand, introducing a place from the

point of view of an outsider. What would a city person notice and feel if they stepped for the first time into the darkness of Zuckerman's barn?

This sense of curiosity, confusion, uncertainty, and speculation can be quite valuable to a story and is often used in genre fiction like mysteries, where the powers of immediate observation (and the question of how reliable those impressions are) are crucial.

Be selective in details to create interest.

As Jane Yolen once wrote, "Remember ... what you don't put down can be as important as what you do." Lao-Tse, in his *Tao Te Ching*, penned, "In a vessel of clay, it is the emptiness inside that makes it useful."

As when describing a character, the fewer things that are pinned down, the more readers are free to flesh out the picture themselves. This often creates a fuller picture, paradoxically, than a detailed description. Also, fewer details create intrigue, as the reader realizes that those being given are somehow significant, having been chosen by the author for a purpose.

Notice how Tolkien's *The Hobbit* (1937) begins with a simple description of place. As we travel into the well-appointed hole, we get a glimmer of the character of the inhabitant.

> *"In a hole in the ground, there lived a hobbit.*
> *Not a nasty, dirty, wet hole, filled with the ends*
> *of worms and an oozy smell, nor yet a dry, bare,*
> *sandy hole with nothing in it to sit down on or to*
> *eat: it was a hobbit-hole, and that means comfort.*

> *"It had a perfectly round door like a porthole, painted green, with a shiny yellow brass knob in the exact middle. The door opened on to a tube-shaped hall like a tunnel: a very comfortable tunnel without smoke, with paneled walls, and floors tiled and carpeted, provided with polished chairs, and lots and lots of pegs for hats and coats—the hobbit was fond of visitors."*

I love those details!

A round door, painted green, with a bright yellow knob in the middle, leads into a comfy dwelling. The few but important details of what we find inside present the character of the hobbit long before we actually meet Mr. Bilbo Baggins.

Pan in from a distant shot to a closer perspective for drama.

A specific technique that helps readers enter into a story, as Tolkien has done, is to move from a broad view of the place (the hobbit hole) to a closer examination of a few features of interest (the round green door, the hallway inside).

Here's an example at the beginning of Jack London's *White Fang* (1906). First, we get a broad fly-over shot, then he zooms in to examine a curious item in more detail:

> *"Dark spruce forest frowned on either side the frozen waterway. The trees had been stripped by a recent wind of their white covering of frost, and they seemed to lean toward each other,*

black and ominous, in the fading light. A vast silence reigned over the land. The land itself was a desolation, lifeless, without movement, so lone and cold that the spirit of it was not even that of sadness ... It was the Wild, the savage, frozen-hearted Northland Wild.

"But there was life, abroad in the land and defiant. Down the frozen waterway toiled a string of wolfish dogs. Their bristly fur was rimed with frost. Their breath froze in the air as it left their mouths, spouting forth in spumes of vapor that settled upon the hair of their bodies and formed into crystals of frost. Leather harness was on the dogs, and leather traces attached them to a sled which dragged along behind. The sled was without runners. It was made of stout birch-bark, and its full surface rested on the snow. The front end of the sled was turned up, like a scroll... On the sled, securely lashed, was a long and narrow oblong box. There were other things on the sled— blankets, an axe, and a coffee-pot and frying-pan; but prominent, occupying most of the space, was the long and narrow oblong box."

Use a variety of senses to develop depth.

Using a variety of senses can create a stronger image of a place, replete with mood, smells, sounds, tactile elements, and, as always, the curiosity created by what someone chooses to notice and report.

Here is the opening page from the fantasy novel *Alphabet of Thorn* (2004) by Patricia McKillip, winner of many awards for her rich prose.

> *"On Dreamer's Plain, the gathering of delegations from the Twelve Crowns of Raine for the coronation of the Queen of Raine looked like an invading army. So the young transcriptor thought, gazing out a window as she awaited a visiting scholar. She had never been so high in the palace library and rarely so warm. Usually, at this time of the morning, she was buried in the stones below, blowing on her fingers to warm them so they could write. Outside, wind gusted across the vast plain, pulling banners taut, shaking the pavilions thrown up for the various delegations' entourages of troops and servants. A spring squall had blown in from the sea and crossed the plain. The drying pavilions, huffing like bellows in the wind, were brilliant with color. The transcriptor, who had only seen invading armies in the epics she translated, narrowed her eyes at this gathering and imagined possibilities. She was counting the horses penned near each pavilion, pelts lustrous even at a distance after the rain, and as clear ... .as figures pricked in a tapestry when the scholar finally arrived."*

Note the feeling of warmth, the implied sea scent of the

breeze, the bright colors of the pavilions, the snap of the billowing tents, the luster of the wet horses, and above all, the sense of amazement by the young scribe who is not in her usual place and therefore all the more observant and impressed by what she sees.

A COGNITIVE SECRET

Knowing the Facts of the Story

*"Anecdotes don't make good stories. Generally, I
dig down underneath them so far that the story
that finally comes out is not what people thought
their anecdotes were about."*
-Alice Munro

*The Idea of the Cognitive Secret: Knowing the Facts of the
Story* happens when our brain focuses its full attention on
something and filters out all unnecessary information.

A story's secret holds the brain's attention. Everything in a
story must be there on a need-to-know basis.

- Do we know whose story it is? There must be
  someone through whose eyes we are viewing
  the world we've been plunged into—aka—the
  protagonist.
- Is something happening—beginning on the
  first page? Don't just set the stage for later
  conflict. Jump right in with something that
  will affect the protagonist and make the reader
  hungry to discover the consequences. After all,
  unless something is already happening, how
  can we want to know what happens next?
- Is there conflict in what's happening? Will the
  conflict directly impact the protagonist's quest,
  even though your reader might not know what

that quest is?

- Is something at stake on the first page? As important, is your reader aware of what it is?

- Is there a sense that "all is not as it seems?" This is especially important if the protagonist isn't introduced in the first few pages, in which case it pays to ask: Is there a growing sense of a not-too-distant future?

- Can we glimpse enough of the "big picture" to have that all-important yardstick? It's the big picture that gives readers perspective and conveys the point of each scene, enabling them to add up things. If we don't know where the story is going, how can we tell if it's moving?

iv.

IMPROVING YOUR SKILL

MULTI-DIMENSIONAL CHARACTERS IN A ONE-DIMENSIONAL WORLD

"Respect your characters, even the minor ones. In art, as in life, everyone is the hero of their own particular story; it is worth thinking about what your minor characters' stories are, even though they may intersect only slightly with your protagonist's."
-Sarah Waters

We create the best characters when we know the depth of ourselves and tap into that depth when we write—using all of our senses.

Character: The most important element in writing.
Plot is important, yes, but characters keep a reader tuned in and reading. Characters set the time and place and make the reader want to keep reading.

- The *what* of a story is not as important as the *how* or the *why*.

How and why characters do what he or she does is what makes people care. Conflict with the story grows out of your characters and should grow naturally.

When characters are well-rounded and complicated, that fact not only shapes their actions; it also helps the reader understand and remember them.

"Honest writing cannot be separated from the person who wrote it."
~A take on an old saying by Tennessee Williams.

3D Characters In A Flat Stanley© World

Flat Stanley, a children's book written in 1964, inspires to address the development of well-rounded characters. Why spend hours learning how to do that? If you are a writer, you know the answer. If you are a beginning writer, now is a perfect time to learn this skill. And if you haven't read *Flat Stanley*, I encourage you to do so and tell him I sent you!

The plot is essential, but characters keep a reader tuned in and reading. Characters make up the most crucial element in writing. They set the time and place and make the reader want to keep reading.

When characters are well-rounded and complicated, that fact shapes their actions and helps the reader understand and remember them. This is where skill comes to bear.

But why spend time improving our skills in creating well-rounded characters?

Why, indeed?

Ask and answer yourself:

Multi-Dimentional Characters ...

1. Why do your characters react to someone or some event?

2. What are your characters' hometowns? How long have they lived there? Do they like it, want to get away, or already miss it?

3. Have they traveled much? Where? Why have they gone there?

4. Have they lived for an extended period in another town? Which town(s)? Why did they live there? Have they lived in any unusual/harsh environments?

5. Have your characters had issues with the law? Was it deserved? How did it turn out? What did they learn from the problems?

6. What culture are your characters a part of? (One country probably has more than one culture, and some cultures span multiple countries.) Are there parts of the culture they dislike?

7. What were the characters' parents like? What were their professions? Are they still alive?

8. Do your characters have siblings? What were/are they like?

9. Do your characters have any other close relatives? What are they like?

10. Do your characters have a mentor? What is he or she like?

11. Do your characters have a best friend? What is he or she like?

12. Were your characters ever married? Why or

why not? Are they still married? Why or why not?

13. Do your characters have children of their own? If so, what are they like?

14. Do your characters have any other resources to draw on? What is the source of these?

15. Do your characters have someone they wish to impress? Why?

16. Do your characters have someone/something to avenge? Why?

17. Do your characters have an enemy? What caused the issue?

18. Do your characters know other characters? What do they think of them?

19. Do your characters have any schooling? (Or for modern/futuristic settings: did they attain an advanced degree?)

20. Do your characters have any non-game-related special skills? (For example, are they a good cook or an excellent lay preacher? Are they driven to play chess nine times a week, etc.?) Bring these skills into play as you create the character's personality, intentions, and so on. In doing so, you will craft a much more well-rounded person who does more than just sitting around looking bored.

21. Was there something unusual about their childhood? (Were they enslaved, given a kiss by the queen for some good deed, etc.?)

22. Are your characters part of a specific ethnicity

that is persecuted? Or are they part of an ethnicity that receives special perks?

23. What did your characters do before deciding to adventure? (Their skills could be related to a prior trade.)

24. What caused your characters to begin adventuring? Who else was involved in the early adventuring? Did anyone die? Did they earn a special reward or find a treasure, etc.?

25. Do your characters have a scar or some mark? What was the cause? Are the mark(s) visible?

26. Is there a prophecy about your characters? Do they believe it?

27. Are your characters being blackmailed, or does someone have undue influence over them in some other way?

28. Have your characters already had some adventures? What happened?

29. What goals do your characters have based on their background?

30. How did your characters get to be where they are currently located?

Granted, all this information does not usually end up in your book, but knowing it helps give your character depth. It fleshes him out. It gives her reasons to do what she does or does not do.

This list could go on forever, but hopefully, you get the point. And if you have children or grandchildren, ask them if they know *Flat Stanley*. He's a cool guy.

A Story Versus "Stuff That Happens"

A story is designed, from beginning to end, to answer a single over-arching question.

We know this, but it often proves maddeningly tricky when we try to tell a story.

TIPS FOR APPLYING AN EMOTIONAL FILTER

*"No tears in the writer, no tears in the reader.
No surprise for the writer, no surprise for the
reader."*
~Robert Frost

When applying an emotional filter …
Pay attention to verbs.
For example, a verb like "walk" is pretty neutral. But the thesaurus reveals a host of synonyms, not only more descriptive but which carry different emotional weights: plod, march, sidle, amble, glide, saunter, trip, and so on.

Think about the difference in the emotional states of a character who thinks *he walked away from me*, versus *he strolled away from me*, or *he trudged away from me*, or *he skipped away from me.*

Carefully choose descriptive details.
If you are describing a person, for example, it suggests a different state of mind if the character has full lips or ragged, bleeding fingernails.

Go Beyond The Obvious

> ## A cemetery in the rain suggests a pretty gloomy state of mind. How can we get across a similar state of mind if a funeral is held on a sunny day?

In the latter case, the contrast between the setting and the character's emotional state of mind can strengthen the emotion.

During dialogue, keep the reader in touch with the character's emotions by what the character says but also by what he or she is *thinking and doing.*

After every sentence, ask yourself, *how does my character feel about that?* Make sure the answer is clear all the way through. (A character's emotions are likely to change as the scene progresses and the situation changes.)

Focus on a character's worries, hopes, and fears as a way of getting at the character's emotions.

Show how a character interprets or feels about what's going on around him or her. Saturate every sentence with the character's state of mind.

More Tips

1. Find a passage in your own writing that feels flat or distant from the character's point of view. Rewrite the passage through the character's emotional filter. For each sentence, ask yourself,

"What does my character feel about this?" (focus on worries, fears, and hopes), then write it in a way that shows those emotions.

2. Write a new scene for your novel, giving attention to the effect of the focal character's emotions on each sentence and the scene as a whole. Apply a strong emotional filter all the way through.

3. Write dialogue that doesn't express the characters' emotions as fully as possible

4. Describe a landscape as seen by an old woman whose disgusting and detestable old husband has just died. Do not mention the husband or death.

5. Describe a lake as seen by a young man who has just committed murder. Do not mention the murder.

6. Describe a building as seen by a man whose son has just been killed in a war. Do not mention the son, war, death, or the old man doing the seeing; then describe the same building, in the same weather and at the same time of day, as seen by a happy lover. Do not mention love or the loved one.

Now, Revisit Your Character

Believable motivation of a character is driven by that character's emotions. We discover this by knowing their backstory. It also helps with body language and internal dialogue. The glimpse of the despondent character makes us wonder why. When we know that, perhaps we identify with the feeling, and it makes us care.

Let's meet Cyn—a character from my book, *Original Cyn*, in the midst of being fleshed out. Consider what we need to incorporate into her world.

If Cyn's backstory causes her to refuse to act, what consequences does she pay? A true heroin or hero always, always initiates action. He or she is never the victim. The reason for that is? Right! Backstory. They may have been a victim in the past, but they vowed never to let themselves get in that position again. Of course, this process can also be a part of the character arch.

Give This a Whirl

I included exercises in this book because you and I both know that we must act on what we learn, or we don't learn it. When I give instruction in person, I get the eye rolls and the suppressed sighs, so I feel like I must convince you to take action here— while also letting you know these exercises are effective. That's why I make sure to tell you about them.

Work with me here, and spend a couple of minutes on the following before reading further. I promise it will not take long and will be relatively painless.

Tips For Applying An Emotional Filter

Your Action Steps

1. Take a minute and jot down at least one yearning—longing—you have. You can do this on another piece of paper or in the margins of this book.
2. Now, list a couple of sensory reactions you have to that yearning.
3. Next, list a couple of things you do to fulfill this yearning. How do you react as a result of that action?

Everyone, whether fictional or not, longs for something. Our yearning/longing is what allows us to express our deepest emotions. At times, it demands that we do. Our yearning can be what we want, but it can also be about something we don't want. Our fictional characters must also yearn for something or fear something, or …

We can't plunge our protagonist or our antagonist into action unless deep psychological needs are clear and powerful unresolved goals, both external and internal, are established. If you don't know what those are, there are ways to discover that—by getting inside your character and your character getting inside you. I don't mean just in your head; I mean in your body. Continue to work to discover more and deeper ways to do that—and in a much more profound way.

Our characters are no different than we are. In fact, our characters actually share our DNA. They are a part of us, even those parts we shove down and hide in the closet of our souls or act like aren't there. We birth those characters, so they take on a life of their own and tell US what they will do or not do, or long for or detest, despite our best efforts.

Our characters must act as a result of this yearning, or refuse to react, as the case may be.

Our story <u>must</u> include that character arch—that moment of possibility. The story begins, moves gradually, then all at once.

Just like the *Fault in Our Stars* (John Green, 2012). When Green wrote this delicious little romp, "As he read, I fell in love the way you fall asleep: slowly, and then all at once."

First, You Dig a Hole. The Story is the Attempt to Climb Out of It.

When we create a multi-dimensional character, fully fleshed out, that allows us to not only shape them but to understand their actions. Talk with your character like you are sitting at the dining room table with them. Remember the iceberg principle. Don't hit your reader over the head with too much information and background about your character. Know your character, but let her or his actions reflect that 99% of what the reader knows about your character is beneath the water.

How Do I Do That?

We do that by building our character through *sensory detail*.

Since our own longings give rise to our characters in one

way or the other, we have to learn to tap into our own senses. Once again, we do that to become aware of our environment, so we can sense it and describe it.

- What do I see?
- What do I smell?
- What do I touch?
- What do I hear?
- What do I taste?

You know all these, but now we are going to add one more—the character's emotion. How might the person feel? In her book, *The Power of Body Language* (2007), Tanya Reiman lists seven universal emotions:

- Surprise
- Fear
- Anger
- Sadness
- Disgust
- Happiness
- Contempt

At one time or another, we have experienced all these emotions. The trick is to have your character experience all of these feelings from their point of view, too. Ask your characters the tough questions they may not want you to ask them. Force them to share their inner hurts and pains. This guides you to discover their temperament and what motivates them.

You will find the people in your story in your friends and

relatives, in newspapers, in movies, in other books, and from that part of your own eccentric mind. Blend it all up. Internal and external traits build on your character's personality and emotional state.

Writers often have trouble creating believable, unusual characters.

Instead—

- We make cookie-cutter, stereotypical people and bore our readers.
- We conduct extensive research. Research by itself won't fix the problem. Why? Because the most important element for creating characters with emotion and psychological depth— wishes, feelings, passions, depth, and vision reside within you—*the writer.*
- We resist the elements that help us develop multi-faceted, exciting characters.
- We fail to connect our inner world with the outer world we create.

It takes more than structure to make our writing and characters come to life. Before our characters can stand out from all the others, we must tap into our inner selves while we create our characters. We must be present inside our characters and in our writing, or our story will not be successful, for it will lack depth. Our readers must hear our voice as the narrator— not some detached fact teller. We must become our characters emotionally.

We must create characters that express all the various voices we have within us.

We, the writer, make the difference between a lackluster character portrayer and a character with a fresh, unique voice.

For instance, we know everything we need to know about psychological killers through the everyday occurrences of our lives.

We discuss them at Thanksgiving dinner.

We see or hear of them interacting in their usual lives and feel their tension.

We discover them as people who take grudges seriously.

If you vacuum up thriller novels or know someone in your life especially voracious about them ... you already know that hate, envy, and greed make life worth living! Even negative emotions create motivation. Shame, feeling unloved, and fear cover the core issue of powerlessness.

Here is the secret I promised you earlier. We create the best characters when we:

1. *Know ourselves,*
2. *Know* the *depth of ourselves, backward* and *forward.*
3. And with total, yes, sometimes, scary honesty, we must tap into that depth when we write.

But ... how in the world do we do this?

My first inclination is to say, "Any ol' way we can!" And that's true, but this is truer:

- We must make ourselves vulnerable. If we are not willing to do this, we cheat our characters out of real-life personalities, and we cheat our readers out of the same.
- We must take risks.
- We must explore our inner selves.
- We must delve into the parts of ourselves that are the most vulnerable—our own life experiences—particularly those painful or delightful parts of our childhood.
- When we approach that more vulnerable part of ourselves, we must not stop. We must not blink. We must write through the pain, the discomfort, and the desire to avoid, at all costs.
- Instead, we will write right through that part of our history, thereby giving life to our characters.

When we do so, we unlock our own sensory recall and transform our experiences, feelings, highs, lows, pains, and joys into unique, powerful, believable, original characters who are capable of touching the hearts of our readers.

Easy to say—not always easy to do, but oh, so vital.

EXPLORING YOUR CHARACTER'S PAST

Why the Past is Never Dead

"We tell ourselves stories in order to win."
-Joan Didion

Guess what?

The past is never dead—actually, it's not even the past.

Whether a writer realizes it or not, she and he bring ghosts from their own pasts into their personal and professional relationships—including their writing. Likewise, so do our characters. They bring ghosts from their pasts into plots. For a writer to develop their characters well, they must set these ghosts free—both their own and those of their characters— that, by the way, are often quite similar.

How do we do that? By bringing them to conscious thought, out of darkness and into the light.

Most writers know it is essential for them to know:

- Their character's childhood
- Their emotional experiences
- Their family and life circumstances

What we often don't realize is before the backstory of our character, it is critical that we build *our own backstory*.

After all, you can't help your characters if you aren't willing to get to know yourself.

If your character has no backstory, they have no character. Without our backstory, *we* have no character.

Exploring Your Past and Starting Over

Think of a scene or a story you are writing or planning to write.

- Recall a time or a scene that illustrates your characters interacting with one another.
- How do their words make you feel?
- Does this scene remind you of a similar scene in your life where you might have experiences?
- How did you feel?
- Where in your body did you feel it?
- What color was the feeling? Feel free to refer to the earlier chapter in the book, where we delved into color.
- Make a note of those characters affected.

When we start to recall our past, we discover a wealth of material just waiting for us.

Go Back in Time

Sit in a quiet place. Relax. Take several slow, deep breaths. Now write about how you felt coming in the door after school. How did you expect to be greeted, and by whom?

Did you feel happy? Fearful? Sad?
What did you talk about? What games did you

play?

What did you smell? Hear? Touch? Taste?

Write your memories and see what they reveal about who you were and who you've become. Remember, once you start, keep the pen moving.

As you answer these questions, keep digging deeper into your childhood memories. There is nobody on Earth like you, so why not put your memories, experiences, and personal passions into your characters? It is raw material.

Fleshing Out Your Characters' Pasts

Record the basics, height, weight, skin type, coloring, hair, eyes. How they walk, talk, eat, smile, their gestures, mannerisms, postures, overall appearances. Are they handsome, ugly, weak, strong, stocky fat thin?

Before you decide which trait to highlight, try to anticipate what important traits he or she will need for his or her role in the plot .

J am a Story Catcher. Maybe that version of my identity came into this world with me. Or maybe she's a figment of my imagination (even though the idea is fun to play with). Regardless of how she manifests within or outside of me, I am very aware, and I hope you are, too, that we are not the ones who decide entirely by ourselves to be that Story Catcher.

I grew up in a community of storytellers and story listeners. Remember, my dad lit up my world with his fanciful stories of the chaos he, as a rough and tumble redheaded, freckle-faced lanky mischievous boy dressed in well-worn overalls and shoeless, got into.

You live in a community of listeners … people in need of story has much to do with whether we become storytellers or not.

I encourage you to pay close attention to what kinds of stories those people need and why. Learn how to mold and shape your stories and what you write to those needs.

In the Inuit culture, people of the Arctic call a storyteller: *isumataq*. A loose translation of that word is "the person who creates the atmosphere in which wisdom reveals itself."

Now …

We've come to the end of this brief but exciting journey. *Wow! That went fast!*

My wish is that you feel refreshed and ready to embrace your next writing project—or your first one.

Story writing and telling are contagious. Once I discovered that writing gave me a voice I'd never found before, I was hooked.

I wish you that same joy.

Please stay in touch.

A GIFT FOR YOU

I believe in always giving back, and I appreciate the time and money you spent purchasing and reading this book, including the short stories.

So, I want to offer you one of my favorite recipes. My family and I lived on the island of Trinidad, West Indies (some people think Wisconsin when they see WI—so I wrote the whole thing out) in the 70s. It did not take long to fall in love with what the Trini's call Fry Bakes. The recipe follows. Enjoy!

Trinidadian FRY BAKES

> 2 cups flour
> Two tablespoons of shortening (Crisco works well)
> One teaspoon salt
> Two teaspoons sugar
> Two teaspoons baking powder or one teaspoon bicarbonate of soda

Sift flour, salt, and baking powder together. Add the shortening, and mix thoroughly using fingertips or a fork until it resembles bread crumbs.

Dissolve the sugar in 1/3 cup water and mix into the flour to form a soft dough. Knead lightly, cut into small thin square pieces, and fry in hot oil until golden brown.

Sprinkle with powdered sugar or leave as is, and eat with jelly and butter.

They are also extra delicious all by themselves.

ACKNOWLEDGMENTS

I hardly know how to approach this assignment, for the list is endless.

So, so many people have walked by my side, led the way, or, to be more accurate, nagged me half to death to write "the next Sidra Smart Mystery."

They walked by my side as I discovered who I am, what I stand for, what I don't stand for, and what I absolutely won't stand for.

Within this list, I dare not neglect the folks who live in Orange County, Texas—Southeast Texas, to be exact. They inspired me, supported me, bought my books, and egged me on to write the next book in the Sidra Smart series, which is set there.

First, Linda and Lisa at L & L Dreamspell, who gave me a chance by publishing my very first book, *Dance on His Grave*. I must, again, thank the late Philip Martin at Great Lakes Literary. Philip expanded my gift of writing exponentially, not only in his editing but also in his gift and love for story. Then, Evelyn Kuntz at White Bird Publishing, who got things done.

Linda, Philip, and Evelyn have all passed this life, yet their legacies live on in the hearts and minds of their authors and the stories shared. Plus, they continue to shine a bright light in my heart.

ABOUT THE AUTHOR

Sylvia Dickey Smith, a multi-published author, writes under the theme: WRITING STRONG WOMEN. Her characters may not be strong at the beginning of a work-in-progress, but by the last draft, they have found their voice and use it not only to help themselves but to make a positive difference in their world.

Made in the USA
Coppell, TX
25 May 2023

17272996R00103